MW00817617

JASON MRAZ

WE SING. WE DANCE. WE STEAL THINGS.

This book was approved by Jason Mraz

Cover art by David Shrigley

Transcribed by Jeff Jacobson and Steve Gorenberg

Cherry Lane Music Company
Director of Publications/Project Editor: Mark Phillips
Project Coordinator: Rebecca Skidmore

ISBN 978-1-60378-111-4

Visit our website at www.cherrylaneprint.com

INTRODUCTION

Even the most incredible of journeys starts with a single step. For Jason Mraz, his life-altering journey began with a single word: no. No touring, no recording, no work for a year. I said, "I want to go to the grocery store again. I want to do my own laundry. I want to tend to a garden. I want to raise a cat."

Mraz came to the decision after a remarkable four years where he had seen his major label debut, *Waiting for My Rocket to Come*, explode off the success of such hits as "Remedy (I Won't Worry)," "You & I Both," and "Curbside Prophet." Shortly thereafter, he returned with his Grammy-nominated, critically acclaimed *Mr. A-Z*, which continued his chart success with "Wordplay." Throughout, his reputation as a tremendous live act soared.

But when he took a well-earned break, something unexpected happened: he rediscovered himself. After a few months, "I suddenly woke up and real songs started coming out of me," Mraz recalls. "Songs that I didn't plan on writing. But that just became a reflection of how I feel and the mood that I was in and these awakenings that I was having," he says.

The result is *We Sing, We Dance, We Steal Things*, his most self-assured effort to date. In true Mraz style, the 12 tunes are wrapped in clever, observant lyrics and strong, engaging pop melodies, but this time they are inspired "by these moments of self realization, self empowerment, and self improvement. I was happy to be able to write an album at the same time I was coming back to earth."

Highlights include the first single, "I'm Yours," a warm breeze of a song about finally giving into love and life's possibilities, set to a lilting Island tempo. A demo of the song leaked out into the world a few years ago and has developed a cult following. "I didn't realize how powerful it was until we went to Sweden last summer and 6,000 people sang every word," Mraz says. "I'd never been to Sweden in my life. I thought,

it's already got a life of its own from the demo; let's give people a great version of it. I feel like we finally got it right on this album."

Another highlight is "Lucky," a simple, endearing duet with new platinum singer/songwriter Colbie Caillat. "I got word that she was a fan and wanted to work together, so I immediately demanded her phone number," Mraz says with a laugh. He sent her segments of a love song that she and her guitarist Timothy Fagan completed.

Caillat then joined Mraz in a London studio where he recorded the album with producer Martin Terefe, best known for his work with Coldplay and James Morrison (who guests on the intricate "Details in the Fabric").

Terefe, along with songwriter/pianist Sasha Skarbek (who co-wrote James Blunt's "You're Beautiful"), also played a hand in co-writing some of the tunes with Mraz, including "Love for a Child," a searing autobiographical tale of Mraz's parents' split when he was five. "I didn't want to share the lyrics," Mraz confesses, "but I just let it rip and it wasn't until playback that I realized how important it was that I needed to write it."

While Mraz and Terefe deliberately kept the music stripped down, they added flourishes that distinguish We Sing from standard pop fare, including a gospel choir on "Live High" and operatic embellishments and a children's chorale on "Coyotes."

"Martin is such a fun guy," Mraz says. "He loves the quirkiness and loves to keep the pace going with little surprises, so he's always willing to try my goofy ideas," such as bookending "Details in the Fabric" with real voicemail messages from Mraz's good friend and sometime co-writer Bushwalla.

The album takes its title from a piece of art by Glasgow-based doodle artist David Shrigley that Mraz saw in Scotland while traveling.

"What I love about mankind is that, yes, we sing and we celebrate and we dance when we're foolish and we steal things," says Mraz, who asked Shrigley to design the album art. "It's hard to have a new idea in music, in fashion, the land we walk on. It's all recycled. I think to say we stole it is a lot more fun."

While on tour in Australia a couple of years ago, Mraz opened his heart and soul to the little miracles that take place every day. "I was in Australia and a package was left for me at the hotel, full of books and CDs: books on Buddhism, books on the Bhagavad Gita, on Christianity, Sai Baba's teachings, and *Autobiography of a Yogi*. All these sort of worldly religious books just appeared, no note—other than 'When you finish reading them, pass them along.'" Mraz dove into the books and world music, which led to his going to India and "just writing things I never thought I would write. To this day, I have no idea who sent me the package. This was one of the many major coincidences that caused me to say: This is who I am and this is why I have taken the time off the road and this is what I'm supposed to be writing about."

For an artist who is so well known for his clever, inspired way with words, it should come as no surprise that many of the songs for *We Sing* were born from a songwriting game he plays with a number of other artists, including noted Texas-based songwriter Bob Schneider. "Bob gives us a topic or a phrase and we have to turn that into a song and email it to everyone." The impressive verbal torrent that spills forth on "Dynamo of Volition"—and once again shows Mraz's unmatched ability to sing at the speed of sound—came from being tasked with using the phrase "blind man's bike." Similarly, "Coyotes," "Butterfly," and "Lucky" all sprung to life after starting from songwriting challenges.

With lessons now learned from sages and prophets in all forms, Mraz is confident he won't lose his way again. "This album…I'm so excited to share it with people," he says, but adds, "I can't see myself getting too lost out there on the road. Every couple of weeks I'm going to go home for a while and I'm going to squeeze my cat and do my laundry, say my thank-yous, and then I'll go out and do some more. There are certain new rules I'm playing by and there's a new me."

JASON RUHL

CONTENTS

MAKE IT MINE

Words and Music by
Jason Mraz

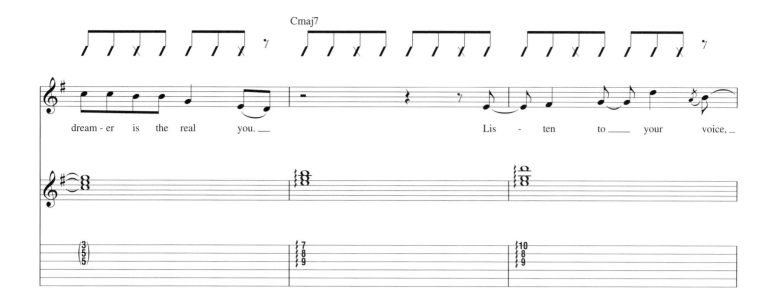

dream-er is the real you. ___   Lis - ten to ___ your voice, ___

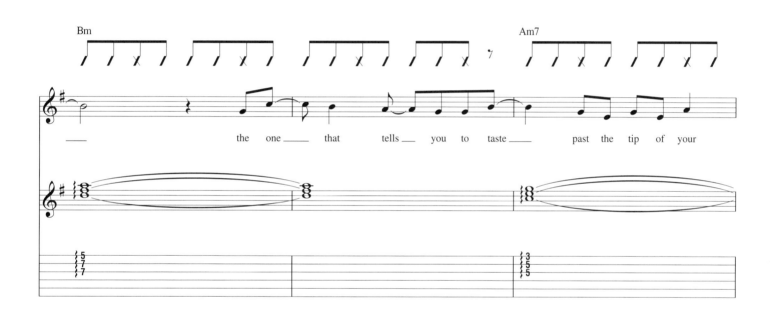

___ the one ___ that tells ___ you to taste ___ past the tip of your

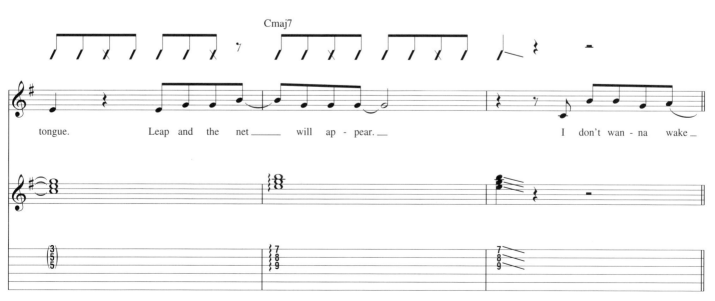

tongue.   Leap and the net ___ will ap - pear. ___   I don't wan - na wake ___

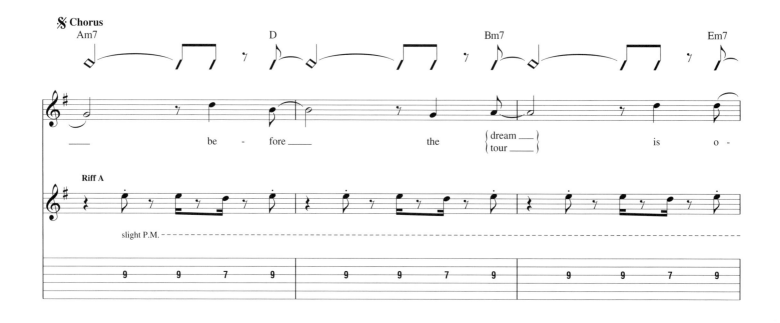

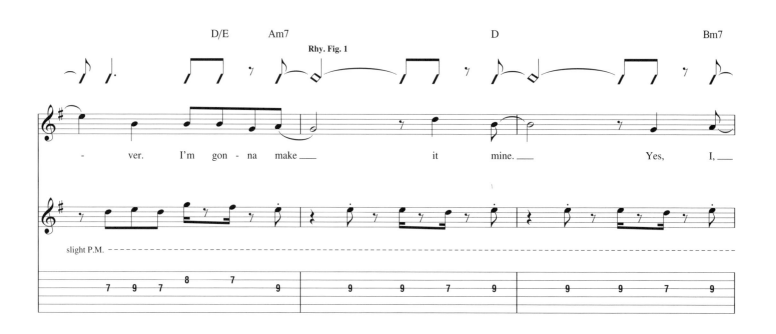

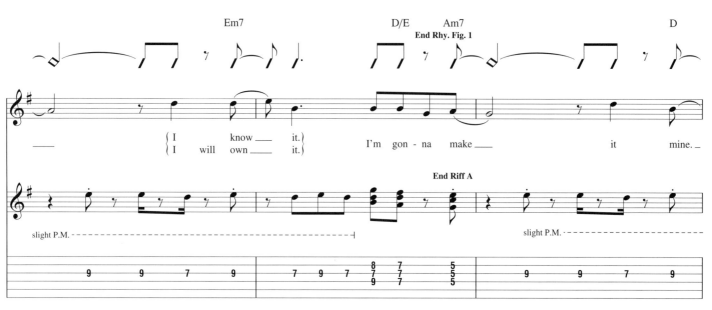

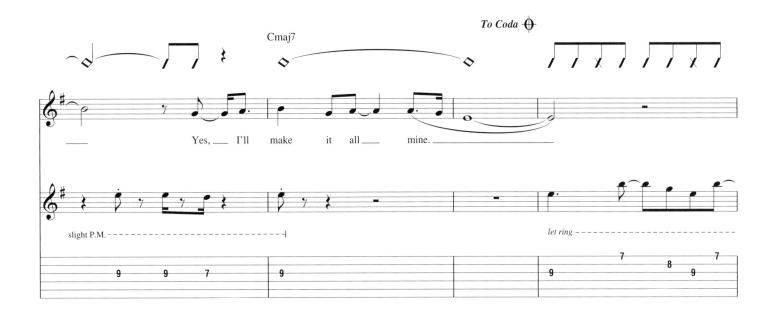

Cmaj7

To Coda ⊕

Yes, ___ I'll make it all ___ mine. ___

slight P.M.

let ring

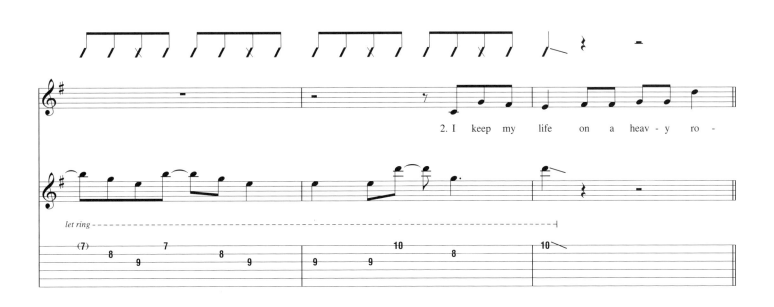

2. I keep my life on a heav-y ro-

let ring

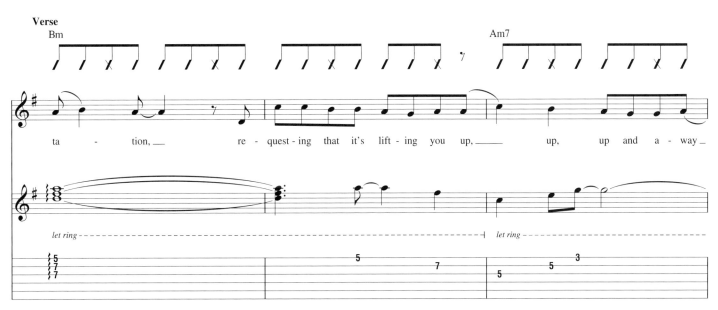

Verse

Bm   Am7

ta - tion, ___ re - quest-ing that it's lift-ing you up, ___ up, up and a - way ___

let ring   let ring

7

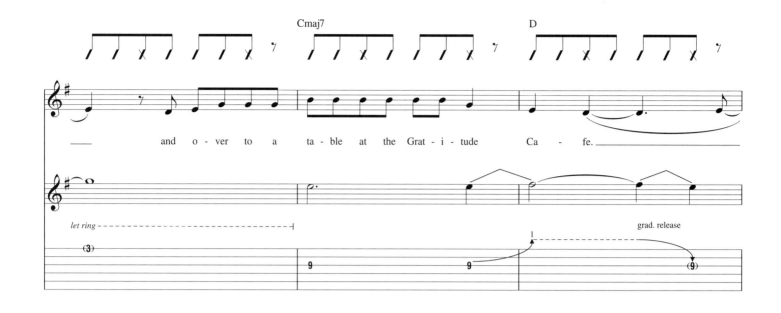

and o - ver to a ta - ble at the Grat - i - tude Ca - fe.

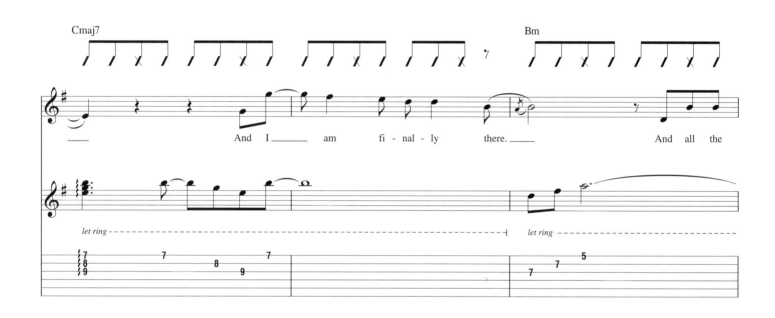

And I am fi - nal - ly there. And all the

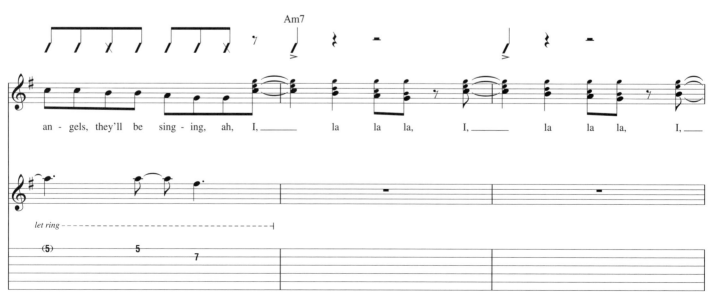

an - gels, they'll be sing - ing, ah, I, la la la, I, la la la, I,

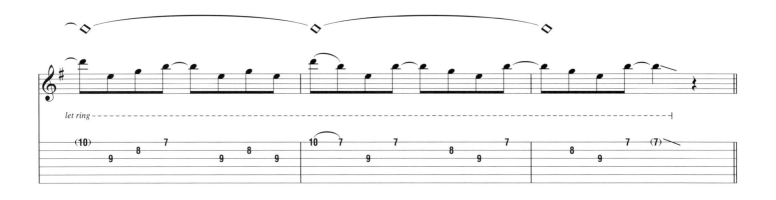

Bridge

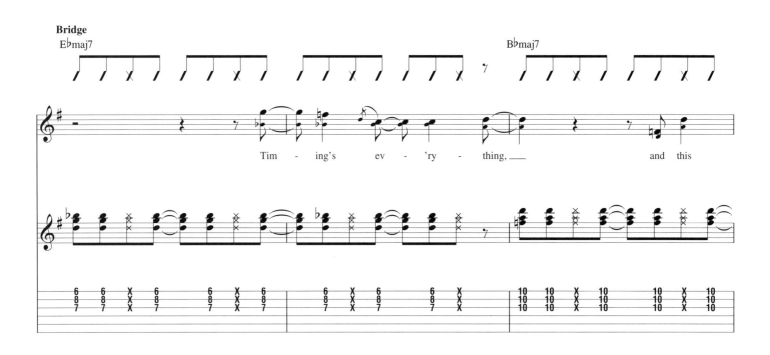

Tim - ing's ev - 'ry - thing, ___ and this

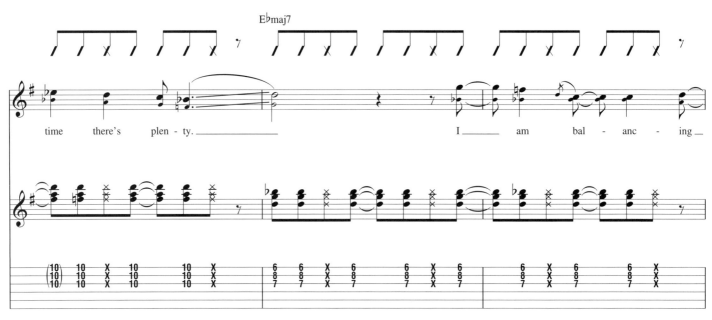

time there's plen - ty. ___ I ___ am bal - anc - ing

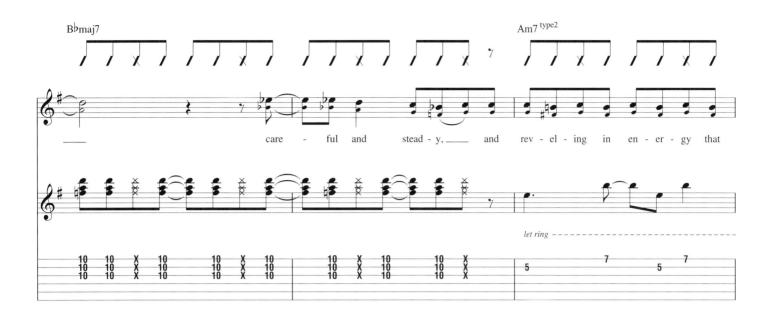

Outro-Chorus

Gtr. 2: w/ Riff A (2 1/2 times)

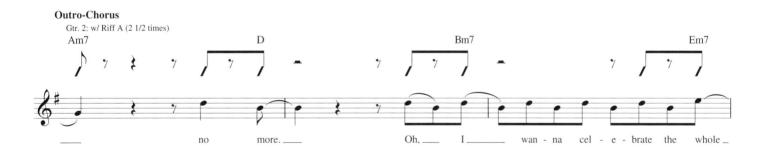

fol - low - ing your ___ joy. I'm gon - na make ___ it mine ___

be - cause I, _____ I am o - pen. I'm gon - na make ___

___ it mine; ___ that's why ___ I will show ___

___ it. I'm ___ gon - na make ___ it all mine. _____

___ Gon - na make, gon - na make, gon - na make, gon - na make it, make it, make it _____ mine, ___

Freely

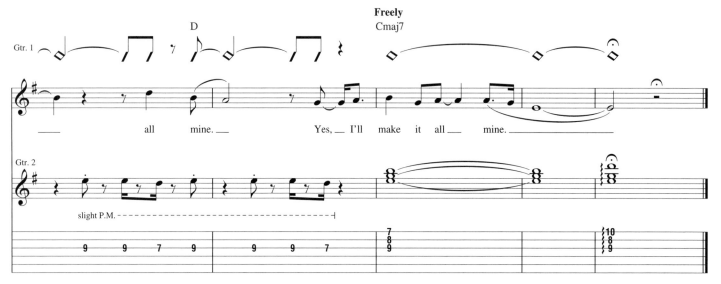

___ all mine. ___ Yes, ___ I'll make it all ___ mine. ___

I'M YOURS

Words and Music by
Jason Mraz

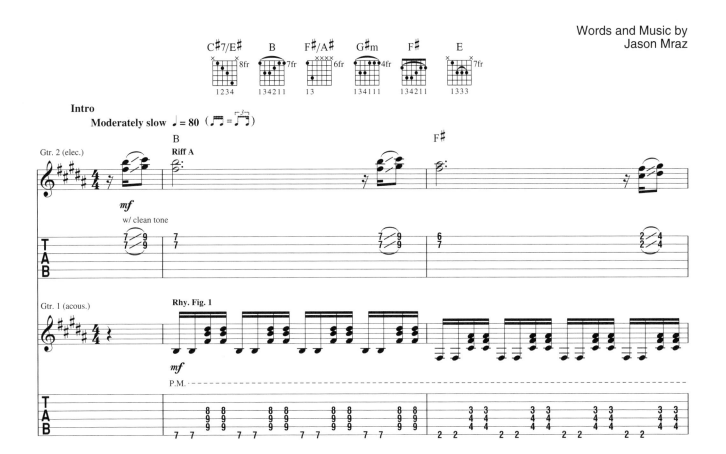

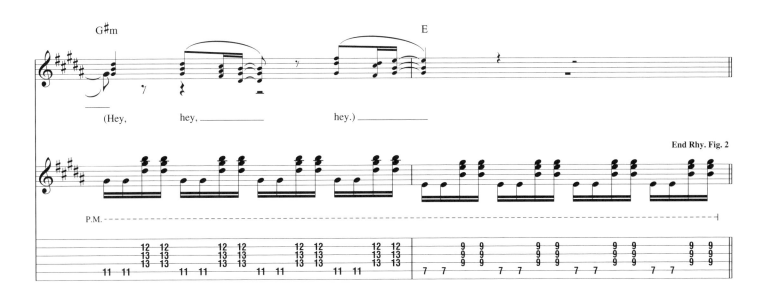

Verse

Gtr. 1: w/ Rhy. Fig. 1 (2 times)
Gtr. 2: w/ Riff B

2. Well, o - pen up your mind and see ___ like me. ___ O - pen up your plans and, damn, ___ you're free.

Look in - to your heart ___ and you'll find love, love, ___ love, love.

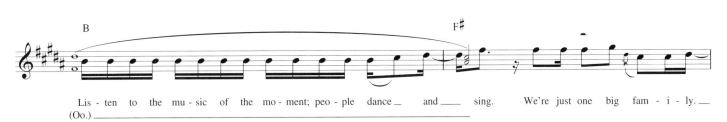

Lis - ten to the mu - sic of the mo - ment; peo - ple dance ___ and ___ sing. We're just one big fam - i - ly. ___
(Oo.) ___

Gtr. 2: w/ Riff C

B   F#/A#   G#m   F#   E   C#7/E#

3. I've been spend - ing

Verse

Gtr. 1: w/ Rhy. Fig. 1 (2 times)
Gtr. 2: w/ Riff A

B

way   too   long   check - ing   my   tongue   in   the   mir - ror   and

F#

bend - ing   o - ver   back - wards   just   to   try   to   see   it   clear - er.   But

G#m   E

my   breath   fogged   up   the   glass,   and   so   I   drew   a   new   face   and   I   laughed.   I

Gtr. 2: w/ Riff B

B

guess   what   I'll   be   say - ing   is   there   ain't   no   bet - ter   rea - son   to

F#

rid   your - self   of   van - i - ties   and   just   go   with   the   sea - sons.   It's

G#m   E

what   we   aim   to   do.   Our   name   is   our   vir - tue.   But

Breakdown-Chorus

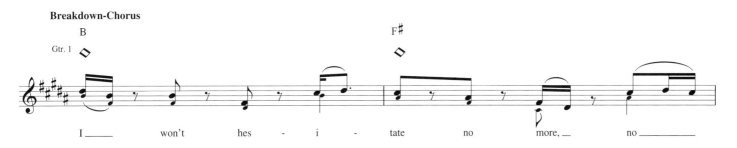

B   F#

Gtr. 1

I   won't   hes - i - tate   no   more,   no

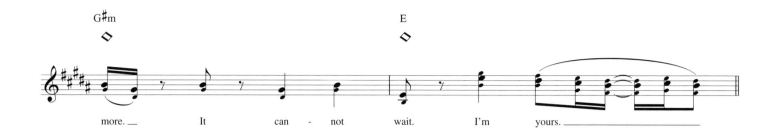

G#m   E

more. __   It   can - not   wait.   I'm   yours. _____

Chorus

Gtr. 1: w/ Rhy. Fig. 2 (2 times)

B   F#

O - pen up your mind   and   see like   me. __   O - pen up your plans and, damn, __ you're __ free.
(I   won't   hes - i - tate   no   more,   no

G#m   E

____ Look in - to your heart __ and you'll __ find __ that   the   sky __ is yours. _____ So
more. It   can - not   wait. I'm   sure. _____ No

B   F#

please don't, please don't, please don't... There's no   need __ to com - pli - cate 'cause our time __
need   to   com - pli - cate.   Our   time   is

Gtr. 2 : w/ Riff C

G#m   E   C#7/E#

                                              Gtr. 1

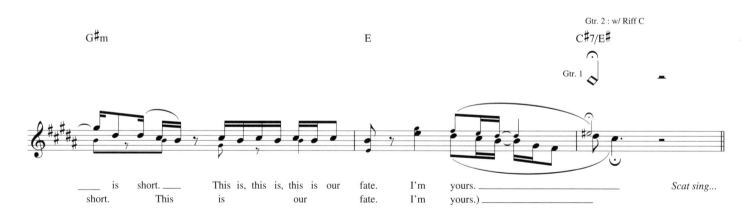

____ is short. __ This is, this is, this is our   fate. I'm   yours. _____ *Scat sing...*
short.   This   is   our   fate. I'm   yours.) _____

Outro

Gtr. 1: w/ Rhy. Fig. 2
Gtr. 2: w/ Riff A

Repeat and fade

B   F#   G#m   E

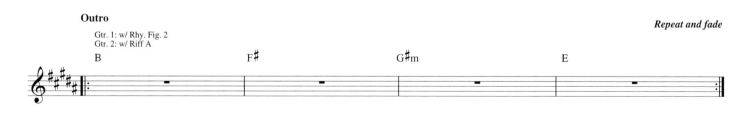

LUCKY

Words and Music by
Jason Mraz, Colbie Caillat
and Timothy Fagan

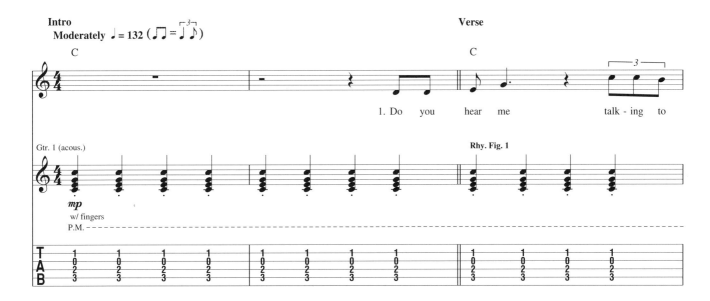

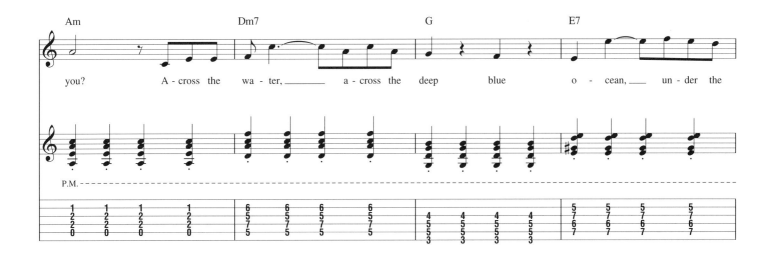

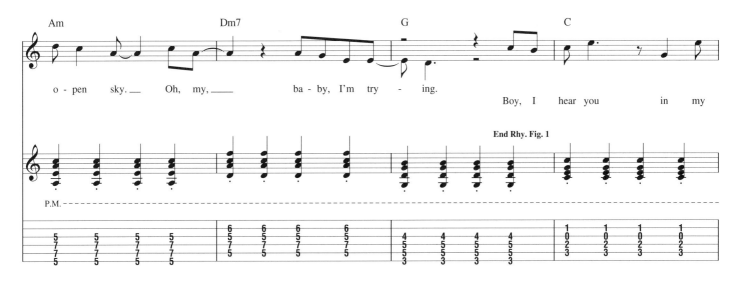

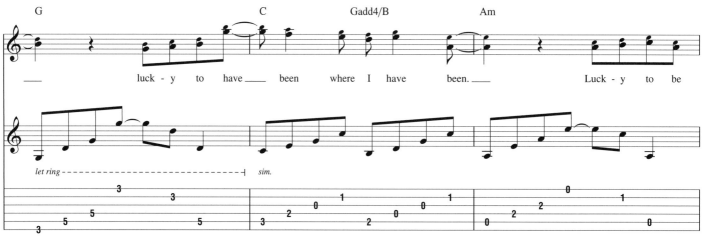

BUTTERFLY

Words and Music by
Jason Mraz

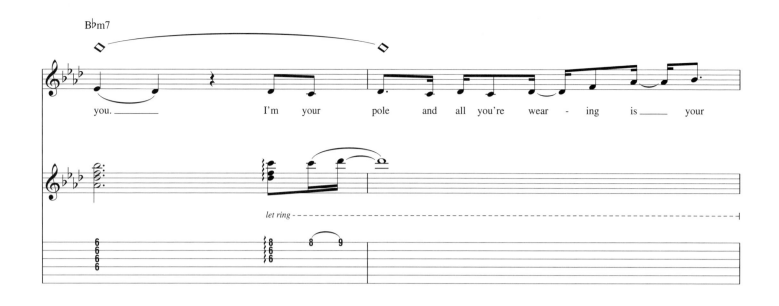

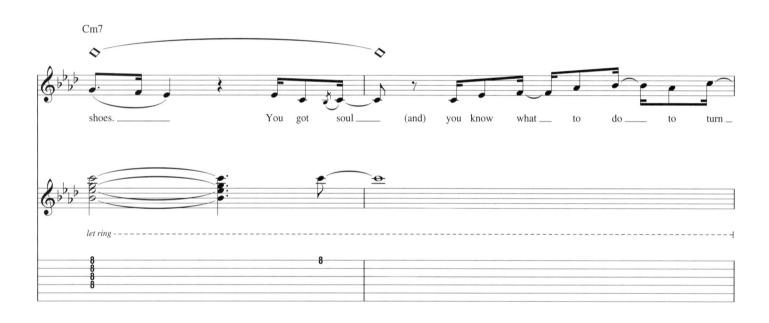

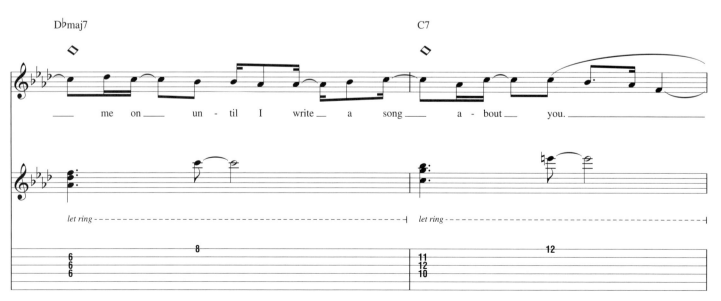

Chorus

Gtr. 2: w/ Riff A (5 1/2 times)

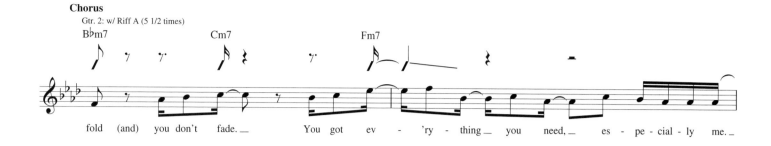

fold (and) you don't fade. __ You got ev - 'ry - thing __ you need, __ es - pe - cial - ly me. __

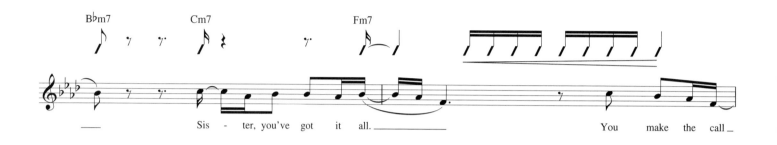

__ Sis - ter, you've got it all. _____ You make the call __

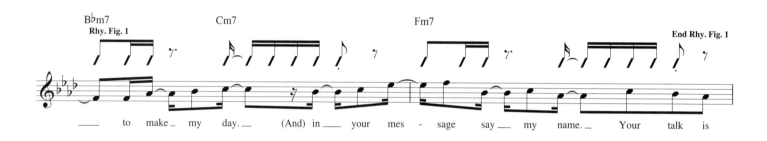

__ to make __ my day. __ (And) in __ your mes - sage say __ my name. __ Your talk is

Gtr. 1: w/ Rhy. Fig. 1 (2 1/2 times)

all the talk. __ Sis - ter, you've got it all. _____

You've got it all. _____

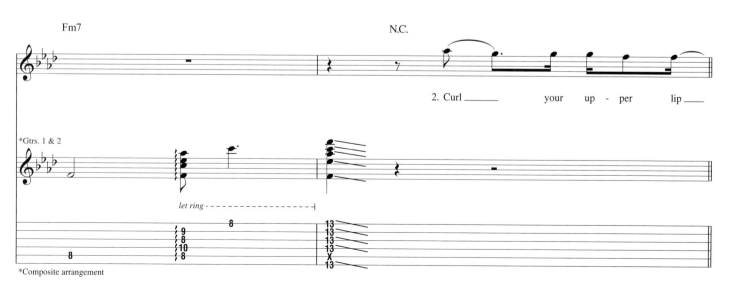

2. Curl _____ your up - per lip _____

*Gtrs. 1 & 2

let ring - - - - - - - - - - - - - - - - - |

*Composite arrangement

28

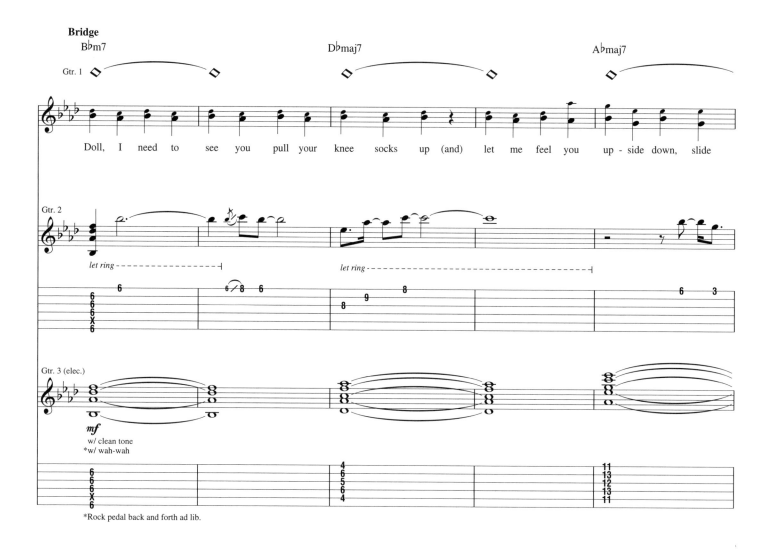

*Rock pedal back and forth ad lib.

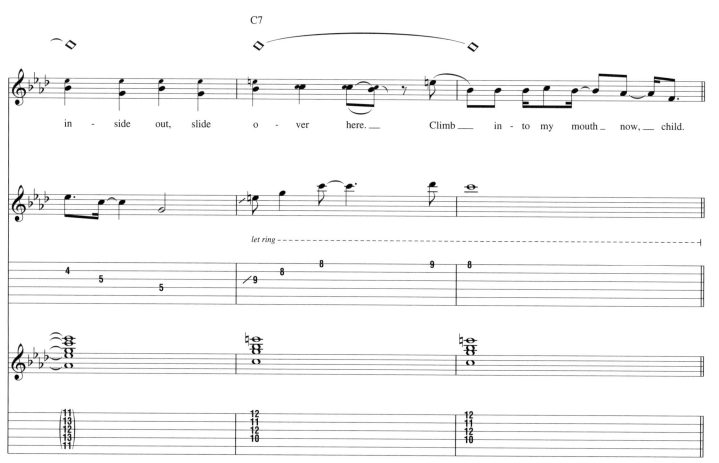

land - ed on ___ my ear ___ and then ___ you crawled ___ in - side. ___ And now ___

___ I see ___ you per - fect - ly ___ be - hind ___ closed eyes. ___ I want to

fly with you. ___ And I don't want to lie to you. ___ 'Cause I, 'cause I can't ___ re - call ___

Gtr. 2

let ring - - - - - - - - - - - - - ┐

Chorus
Gtr. 1: w/ Rhy. Fig. 1 (8 times)
Gtr. 2: w/ Riff A (6 times)

___ a bet - ter day, ___ sun com - ing to shine ___ on the ___ oc - ca - sion. You're an o -

- pen - mind - ed la - dy; you've got it all. ___ And I nev - er

for - get a face ___ 'cept for may - be my own. ___ I have ___ my days. ___ Let's face the fact ___

___ here, it's you ___ who's got it all. ___ You know ___ that for -

- tune fa - vors the brave. Well, let me get paid while I make you break - fast. The rest ___

34

is up___ to you. You make the call. _____ You make the call___

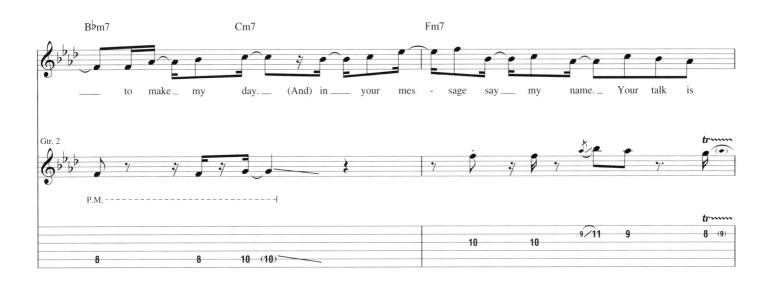

to make_ my day.__ (And) in___ your mes - sage say___ my name.__ Your talk is

all the talk.__ Sis - ter, you've got it all. _____ I can't re - call___

Breakdown

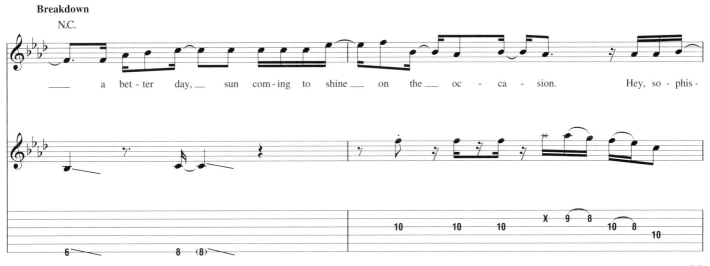

a bet - ter day,__ sun com - ing to shine___ on the___ oc - ca - sion. Hey, so - phis -

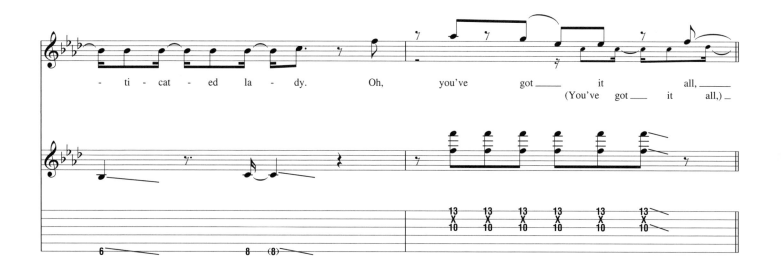

-ti-cat-ed la-dy. Oh, you've got ___ it all, ___
(You've got ___ it all,) ___

Outro
Gtr. 1: w/ Rhy. Fig. 1 (7 1/2 times)
Gtr. 2: w/ Riff A (7 1/2 times)

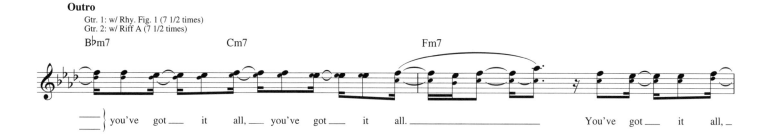

___ you've got ___ it all, ___ you've got ___ it all. ___ You've got ___ it all, ___

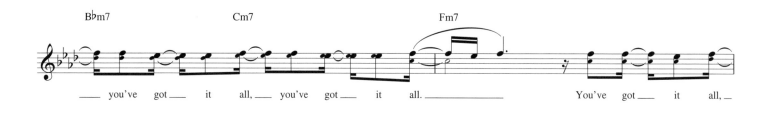

___ you've got ___ it all, ___ you've got ___ it all. ___ You've got ___ it all, ___

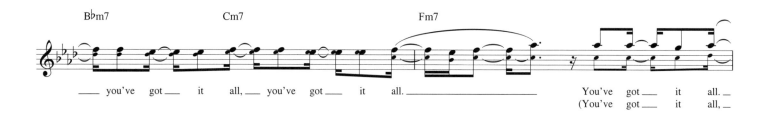

___ you've got ___ it all, ___ you've got ___ it all. ___ You've got ___ it all. ___
(You've got ___ it all, ___

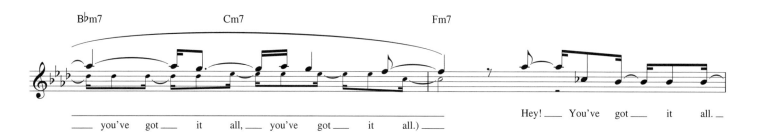

___ you've got ___ it all, you've got ___ it all.) ___ Hey! ___ You've got ___ it all.

___ Woo! ___ You've got, you, ___ you've got it all.

Hey! __ You gots, you gots, you gots, you got __ it all. __

__ Oh! __ You've got, you've got it all. __ Hey! __

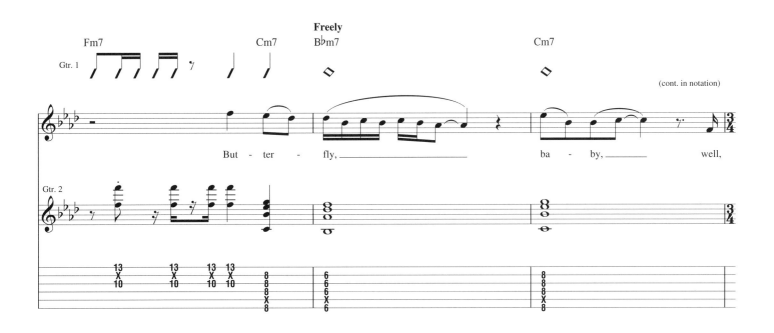

But - ter - fly, __ ba - by, __ well,

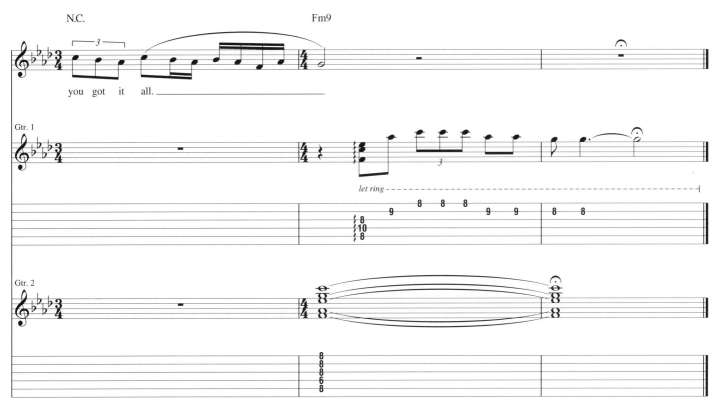

you got it all.

LIVE HIGH

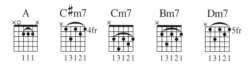

Words and Music by
Jason Mraz

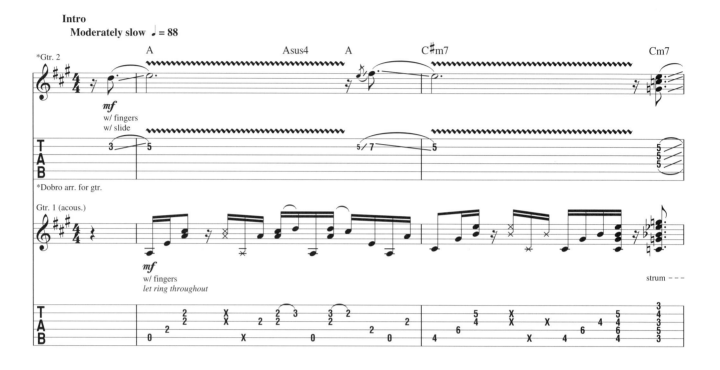

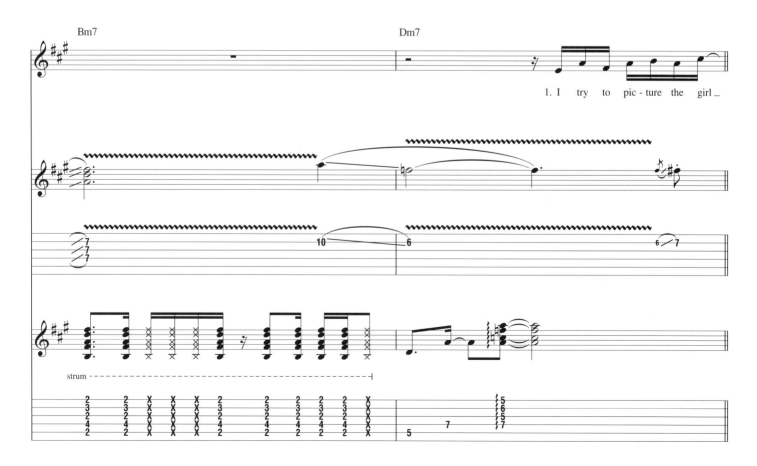

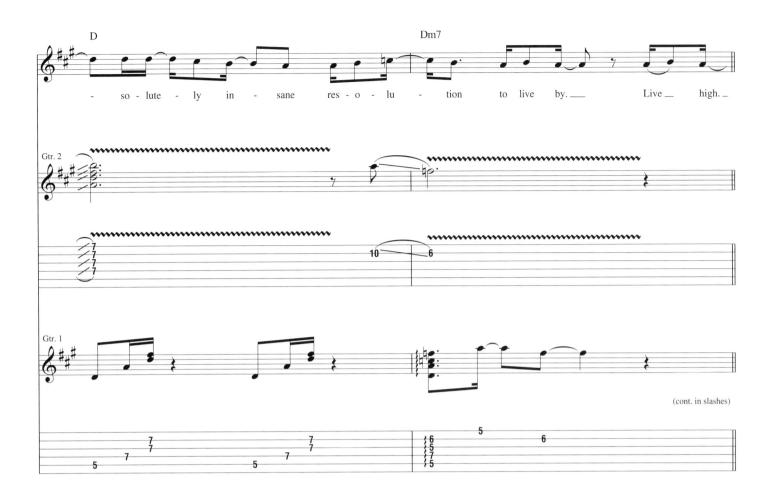

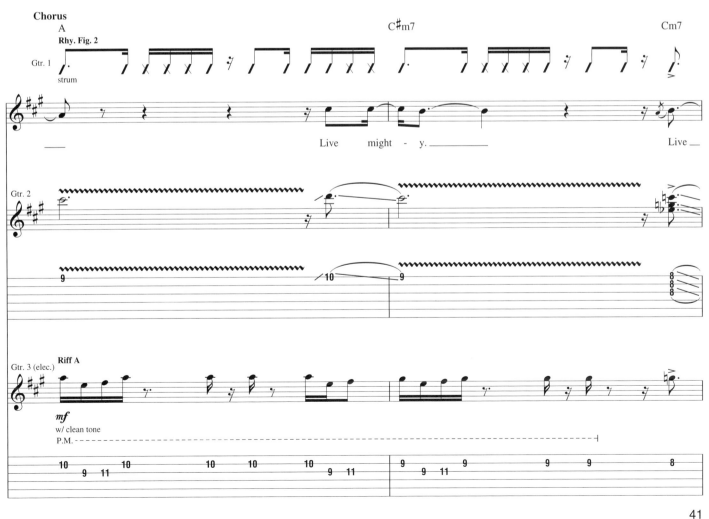

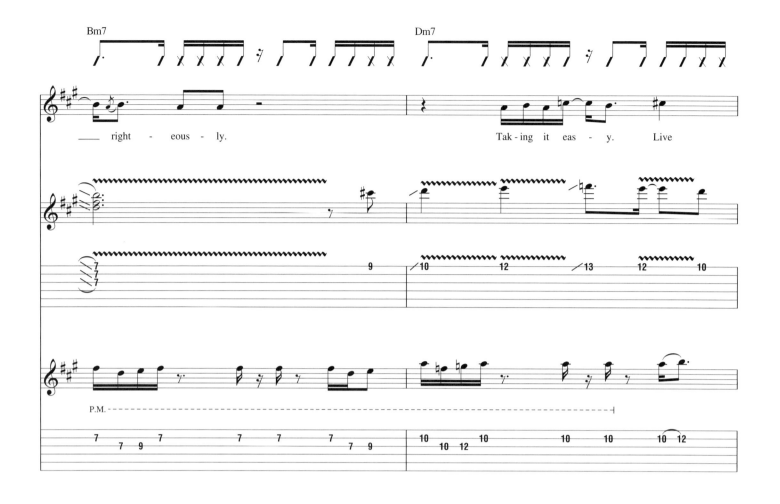

right - eous - ly.　Tak - ing it eas - y.　Live

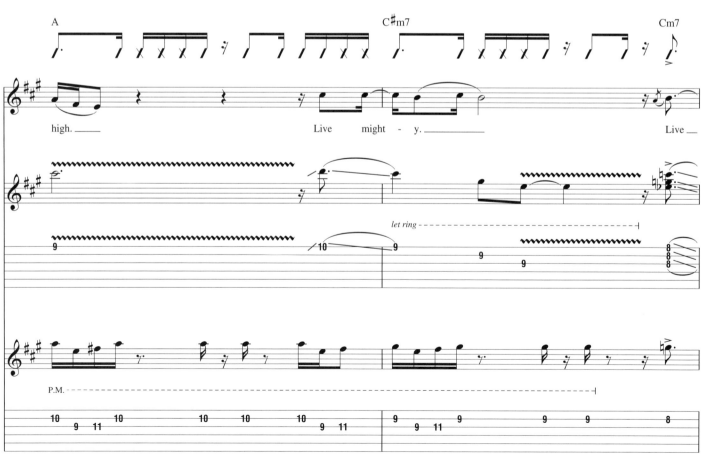

high. ____　Live might - y. ____　Live ___

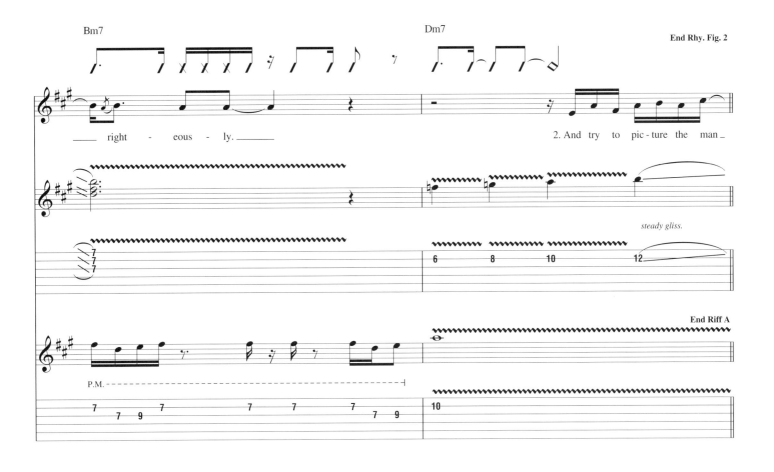

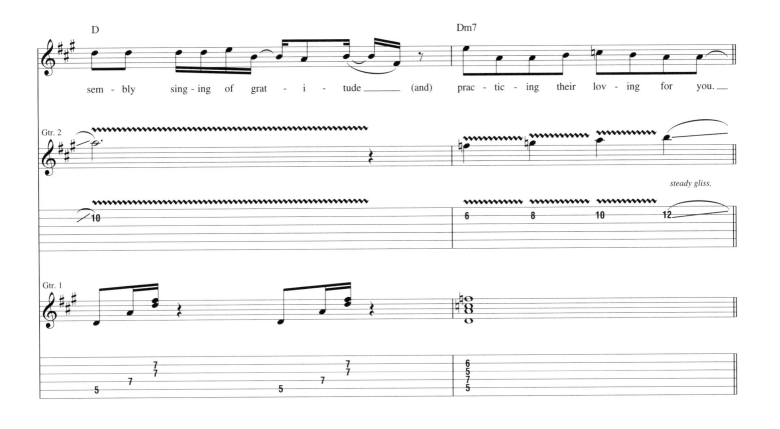

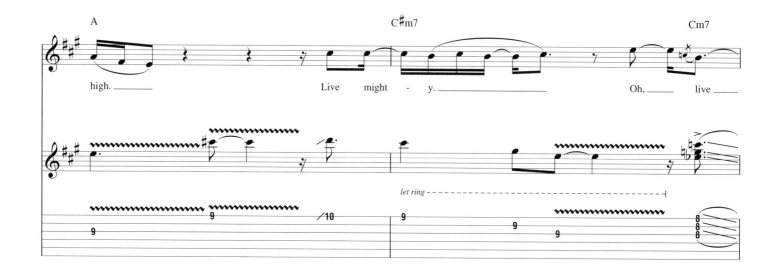

high. _____   Live might - y. _____   Oh, _____ live _____

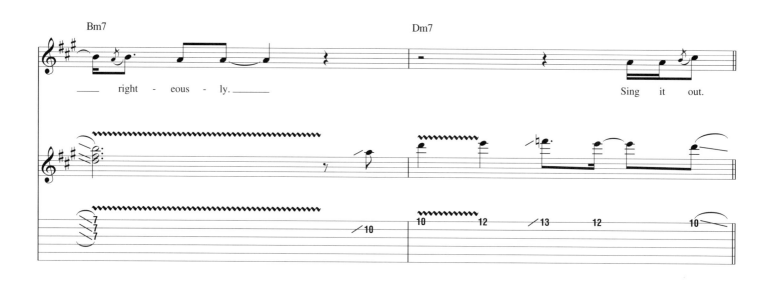

_____ right - eous - ly. _____   Sing it out.

Bridge

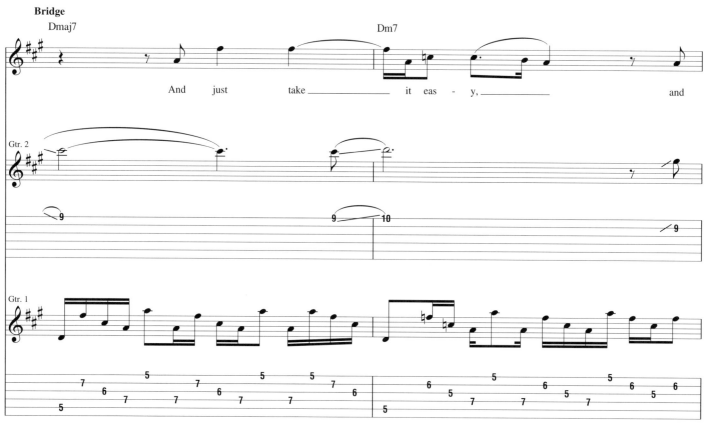

And just take _____ it eas - y, _____ and

46

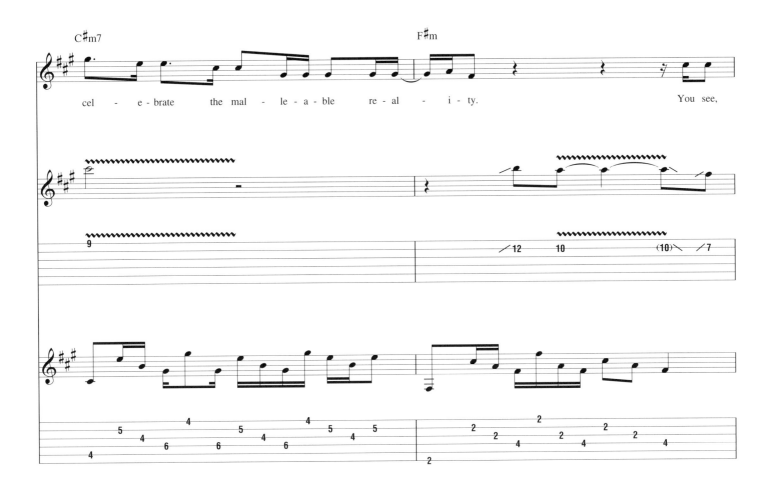

cel - e - brate the mal - le - a - ble re - al - i - ty.   You see,

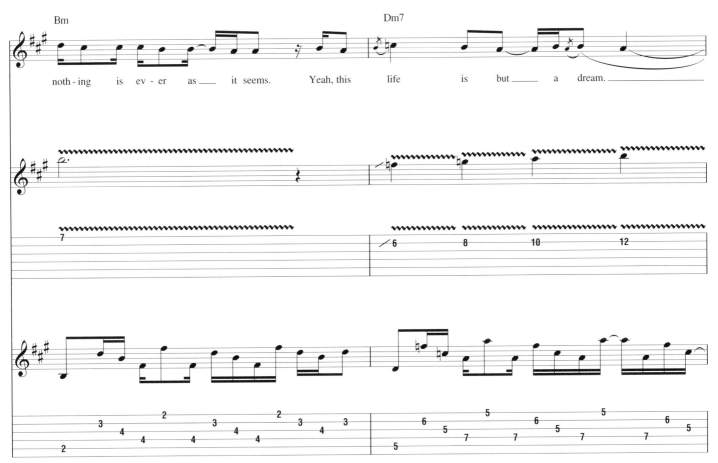

noth - ing is ev - er as ___ it seems.   Yeah, this   life   is   but ___ a   dream. _____

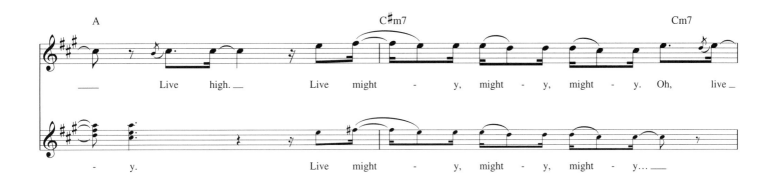

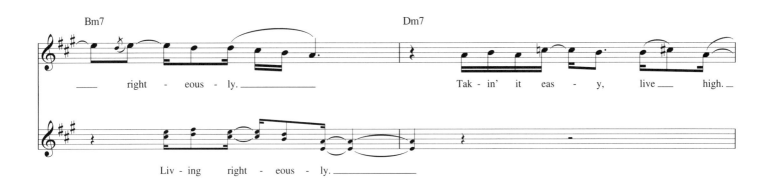

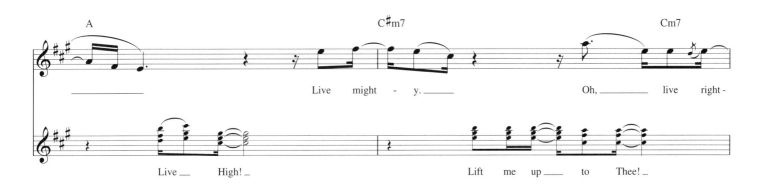

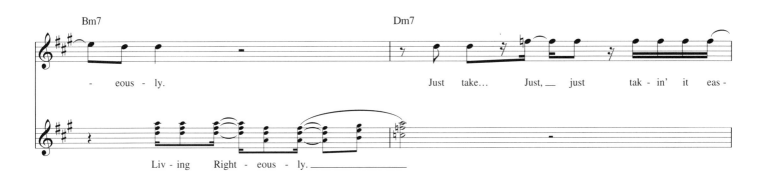

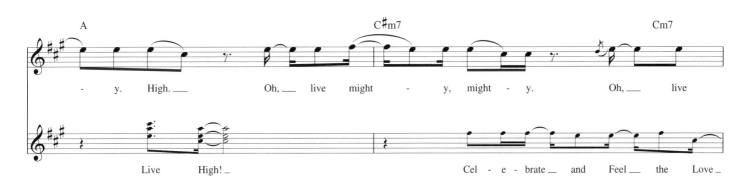

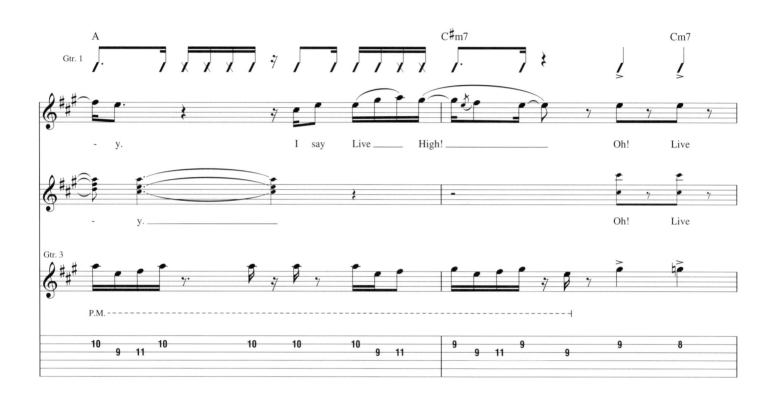

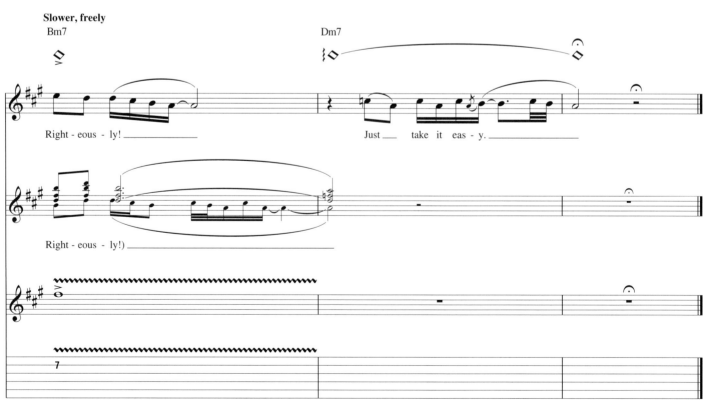

LOVE FOR A CHILD

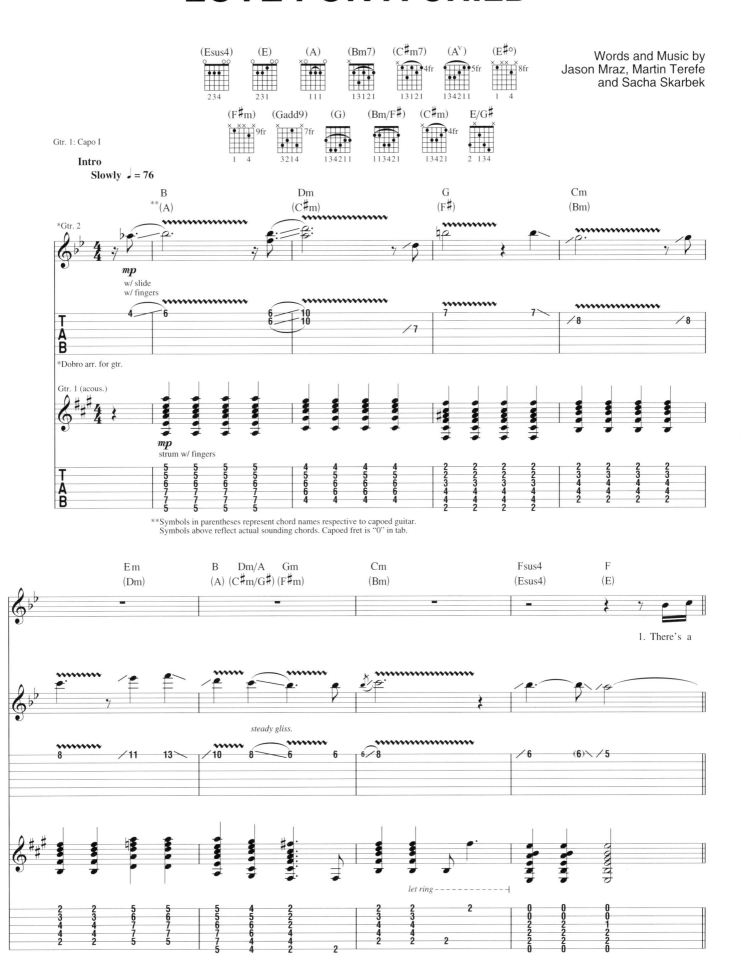

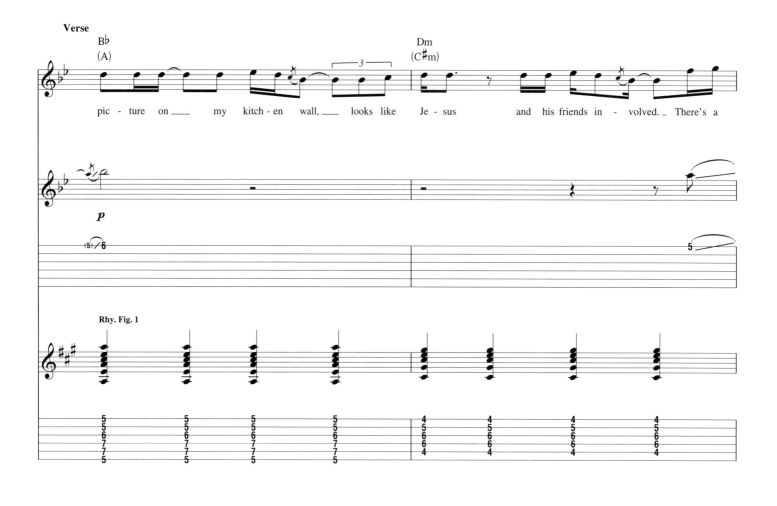

Verse

pic - ture on ___ my kitch - en wall, ___ looks like Je - sus and his friends in - volved. ___ There's a

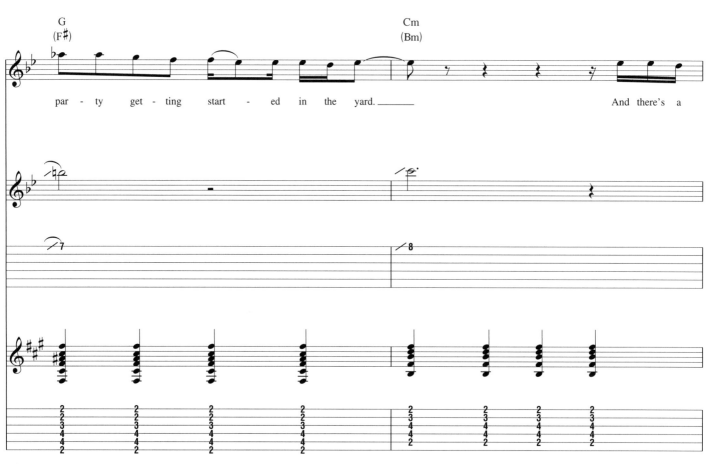

par - ty get - ting start - ed in the yard. ___ And there's a

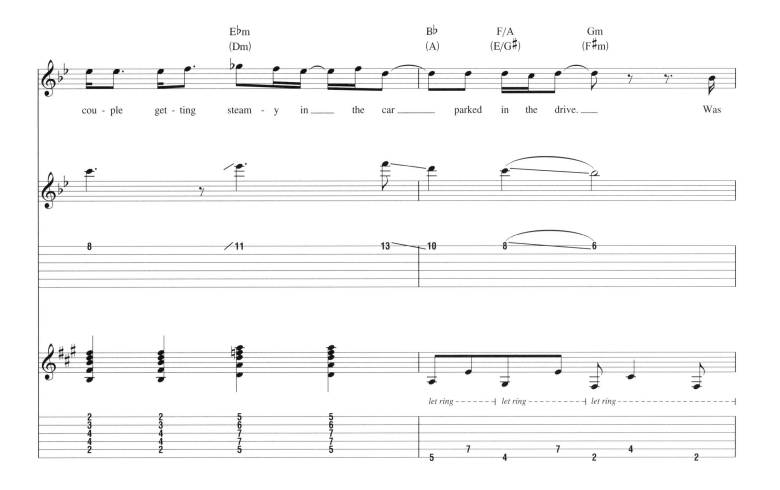

couple get-ting steam-y in ___ the car ___ parked in the drive. ___ Was

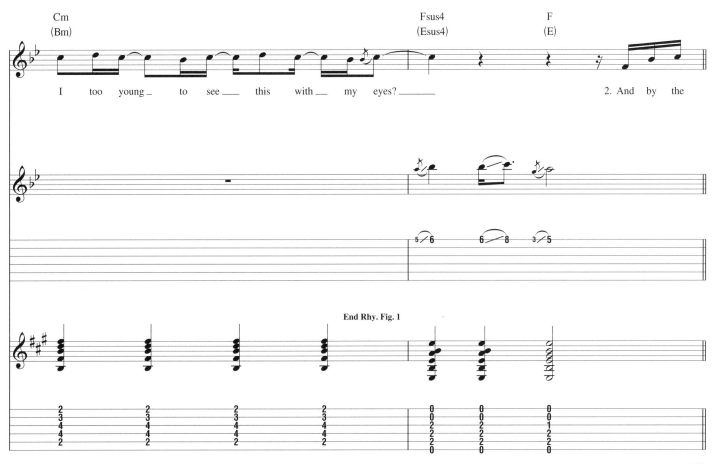

I too young ___ to see ___ this with ___ my eyes? ___ 2. And by the

End Rhy. Fig. 1

Verse

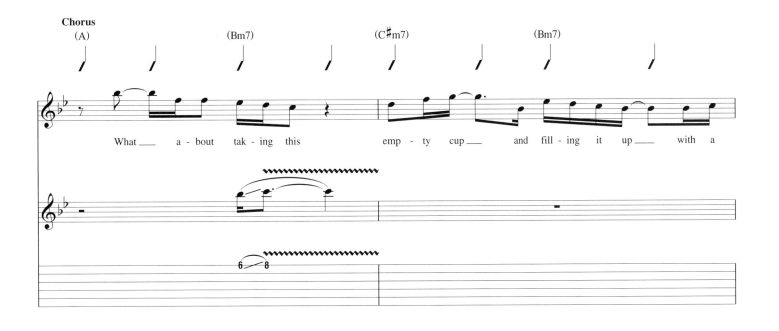

Chorus

What ___ a - bout tak - ing this emp - ty cup ___ and fill - ing it up ___ with a

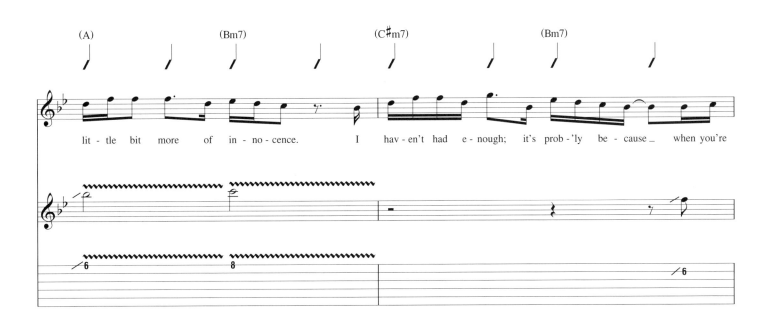

lit - tle bit more of in - no - cence. I hav - en't had e - nough; it's prob - 'ly be - cause ___ when you're

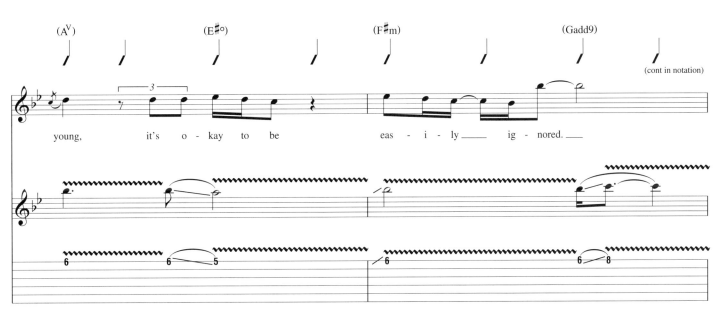

young, it's o - kay to be eas - i - ly ___ ig - nored. ___

(cont in notation)

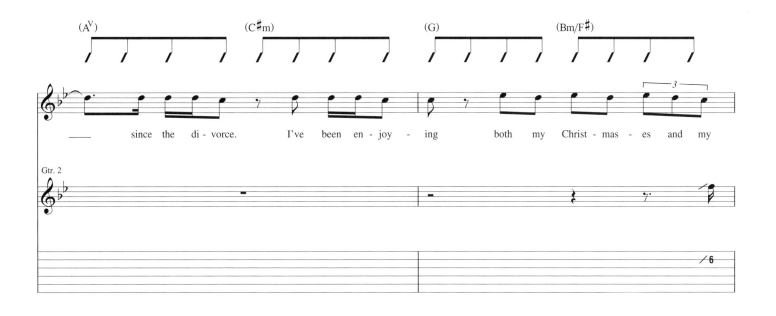

since the di - vorce. I've been en - joy - ing both my Christ - mas - es and my

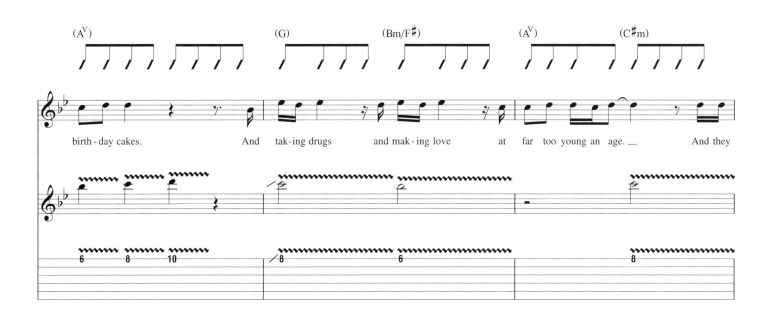

birth - day cakes. And tak - ing drugs and mak - ing love at far too young an age. __ And they

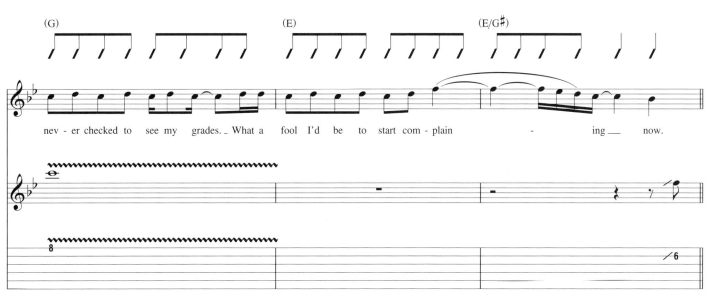

nev - er checked to see my grades. __ What a fool I'd be to start com - plain - ing __ now.

Chorus

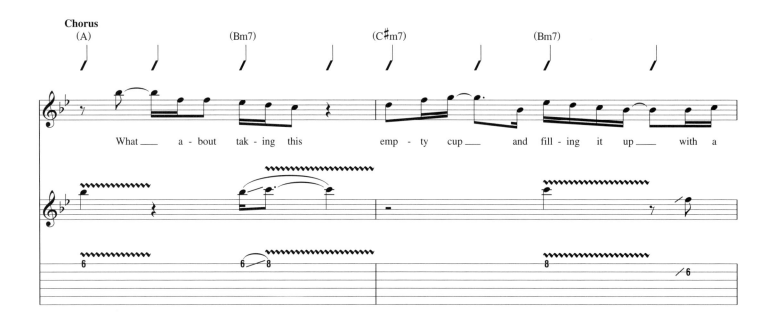

What ___ a - bout tak - ing this emp - ty cup ___ and fill - ing it up ___ with a

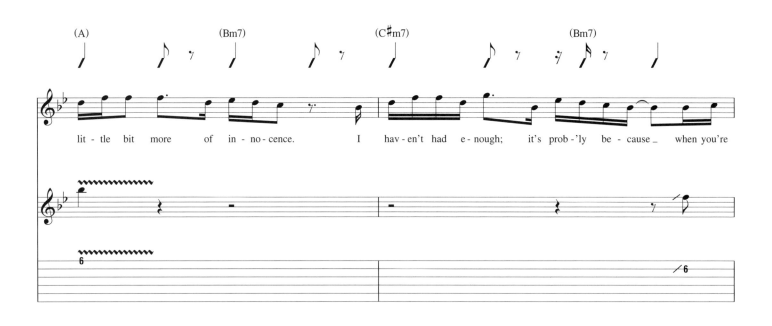

lit - tle bit more of in - no - cence. I hav - en't had e - nough; it's prob -'ly be - cause ___ when you're

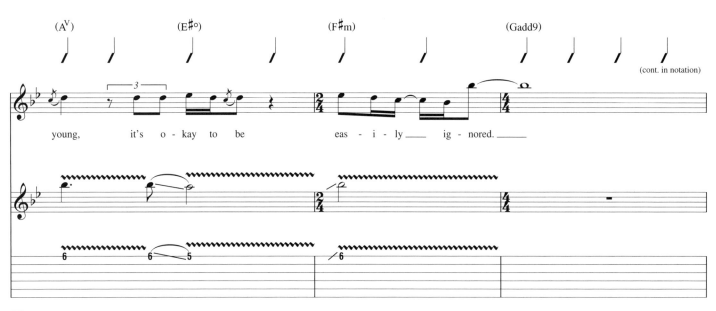

young, it's o - kay to be eas - i - ly ___ ig - nored. ___

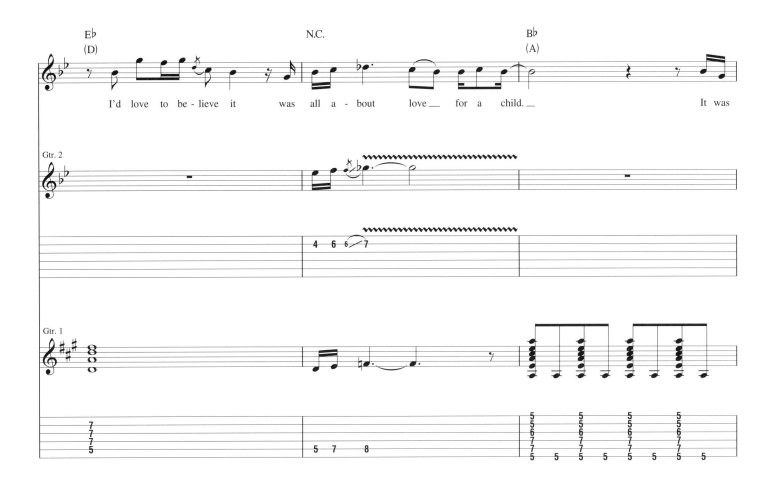

I'd love to be-lieve it was all a-bout love ___ for a child. ___ It was

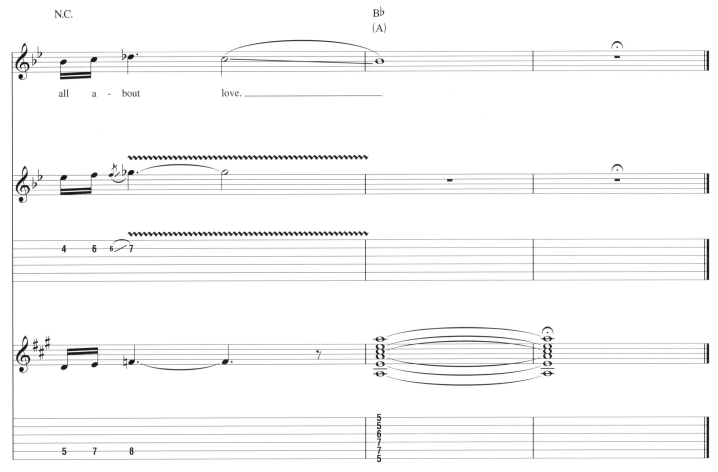

all a-bout love. ___

DETAILS IN THE FABRIC
(Sewing Machine)

Words and Music by
Jason Mraz and Dan Wilson

Capo VI

Intro
Moderately ♩ = 96

*All music sounds 3 steps higher than indicated due to capo. Capoed fret is "0" in tab.
**Throughout song, strum beats 2 & 4 with nails.

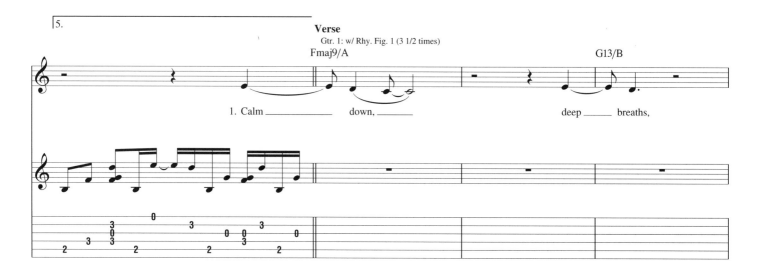

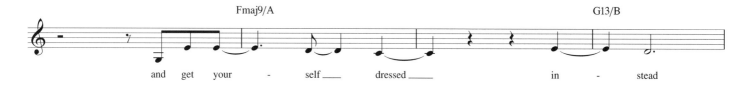

G13/B

breaking your - self up. If it's ___ a bro -

Fmaj9/A

- ken part, ___ re - place ___ it. If it's a bro - ken arm, ___ then brace it. If it's a

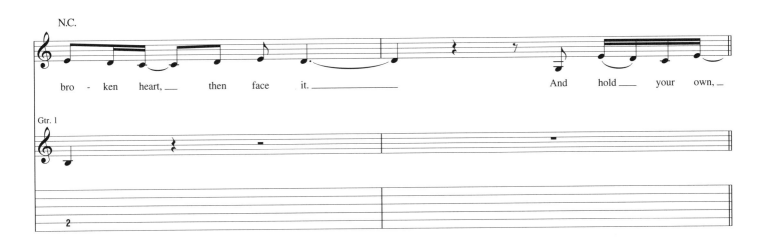

N.C.

bro - ken heart, ___ then face it. ___ And hold ___ your own, ___

Gtr. 1

𝄋 **Chorus**
C   G6/B

know ___ your name, and go your

Rhy. Fig. 2

Am7

own ___ way. ___ Hold ___ your own ___

Verse

Gtr. 1: w/ Rhy. Fig. 1 (1 3/4 times)

Fmaj9/A   G13/B

_____ on. _____   Help is on _____ the way. _____   Stay _____

D.S. al Coda

Gtr. 1: w/ Rhy. Fill 1

Fmaj9/A   G13/B

_____ strong. _____   I'm do - ing _____ ev - 'ry - thing. _____   Hold _ your own, _

✛ Coda

F   G

thing,   ev - 'ry - thing   will _____ be

Rhy. Fig. 3   End Rhy. Fig. 3

F   G

fine.   Ev - 'ry - thing. _____   Are the

Bridge

Gtr. 1: w/ Rhy. Fig. 2

C   G6/B

de - tails in the fab - ric?   Are there things that make _ you pan - ic?   Are your

Am7

thoughts re - sults ___ of stat - ic cling? _____ Are there

C   G6/B

things that make you blow? _____ Hell, no rea - son. Go on and scream. _ If you're

Am7   C/G

shocked it's just the fault ___ of fault - y man - u - fac - tur - ing. _

Gtr. 1: w/ Rhy. Fig. 3 (2 times)
F   G   F   G

Ev - 'ry - thing _____ will _ be fine. Ev - 'ry - thing _____ in no _ time _

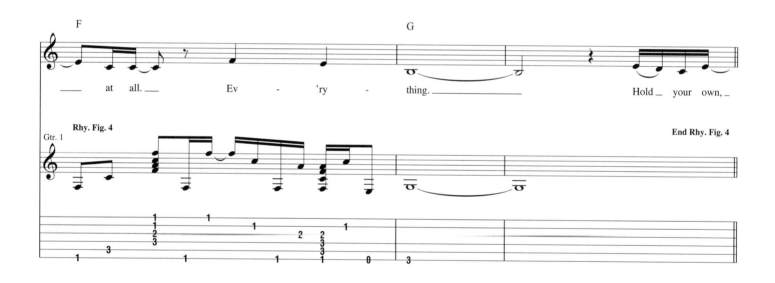

F   G

___ at all. _ Ev - 'ry - thing. _____ Hold _ your own, _

Rhy. Fig. 4   **End Rhy. Fig. 4**
Gtr. 1

Chorus
C   G6/B

___ know _ your name, _ go your

Rhy. Fig. 5

Gtr. 1: w/ Rhy. Fig. 5 (2 times)

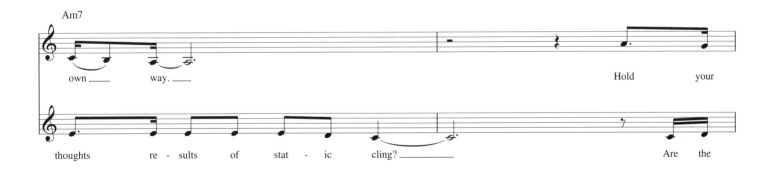

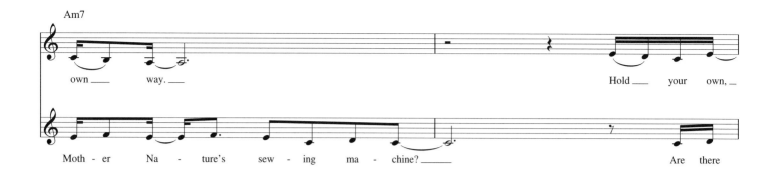

Am7

own ___ way. ___

Hold ___ your own, ___

Moth - er Na - ture's sew - ing ma - chine? _____

Are there

Gtr. 1: w/ Rhy. Fig. 2 (last 4 meas.)

C

G6/B

know your name, ___

go your

things that make ___ you blow? _____ Hell, no rea - son. Go on and scream. If you're

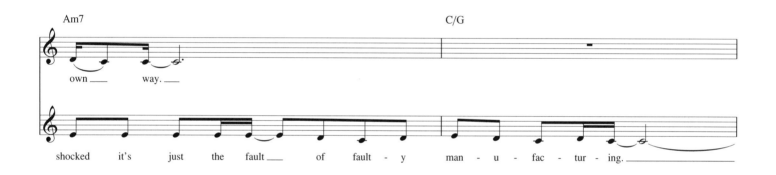

Am7

C/G

own ___ way. ___

shocked it's just the fault ___ of fault - y man - u - fac - tur - ing. _____

Gtr. 1: w/ Rhy. Fig. 3 (2 times)

F   G   F   G

___ Ev - 'ry - thing will ___ be fine. Ev - 'ry - thing _____ in no ___ time ___

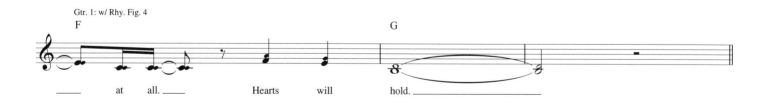

Gtr. 1: w/ Rhy. Fig. 4

F   G

_____ at all. ___ Hearts will hold. _____

Outro

*Gtr. 1: w/ Rhy. Fig. 1 (2 times)   Gtr. 1: w/ Rhy. Fig. 1 (1st meas.)

Fmaj9/A   G13/B   Fmaj9/A   **G/B   N.C.

*Grad. fade   **Played by kybds.

COYOTES

Words and Music by
Jason Mraz

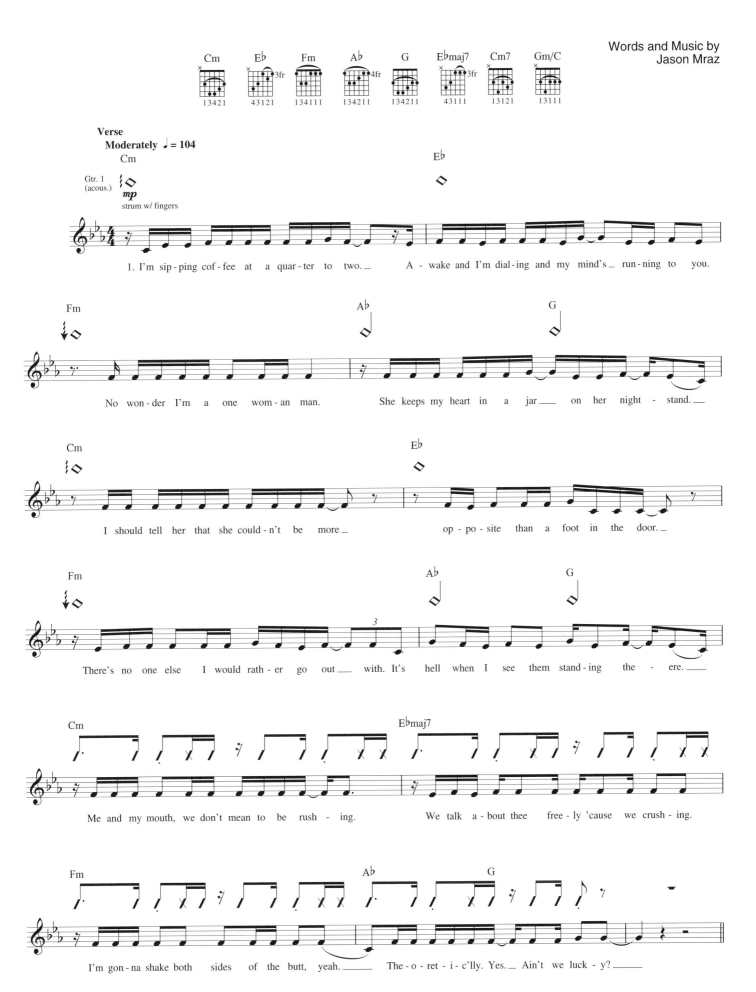

Pre-Chorus

And when the coy - o - tes, they sing in the park,

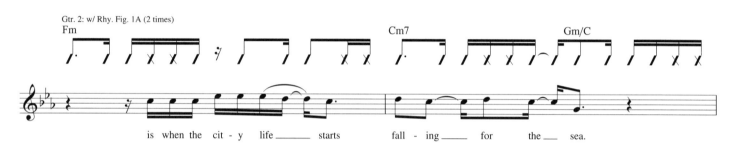

is when the cit - y life starts fall - ing for the sea.

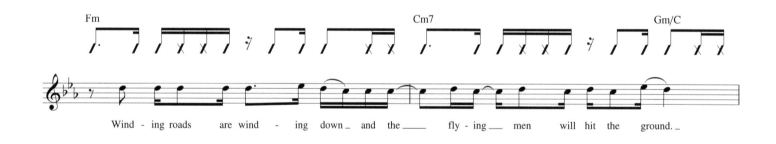

Wind - ing roads are wind - ing down and the fly - ing men will hit the ground.

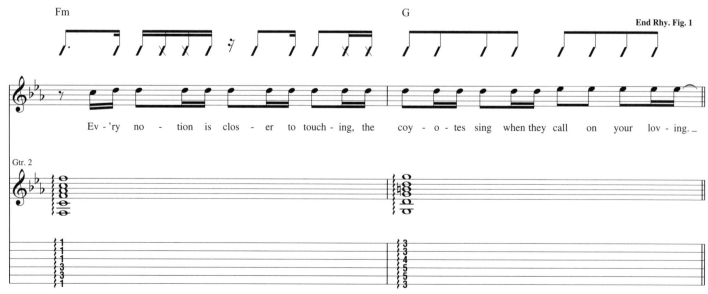

Ev - 'ry no - tion is clos - er to touch-ing, the coy - o - tes sing when they call on your lov - ing.

Breakdown

Gtr. 2 tacet

*Kybd. arr. for gtr.

(Hel - lo.) ___

End Riff A

Chorus

Gtr. 3: w/ Riff A (3 times)

(We're com-ing back for more.___ You know why ___ we're com-ing for you.___ You know

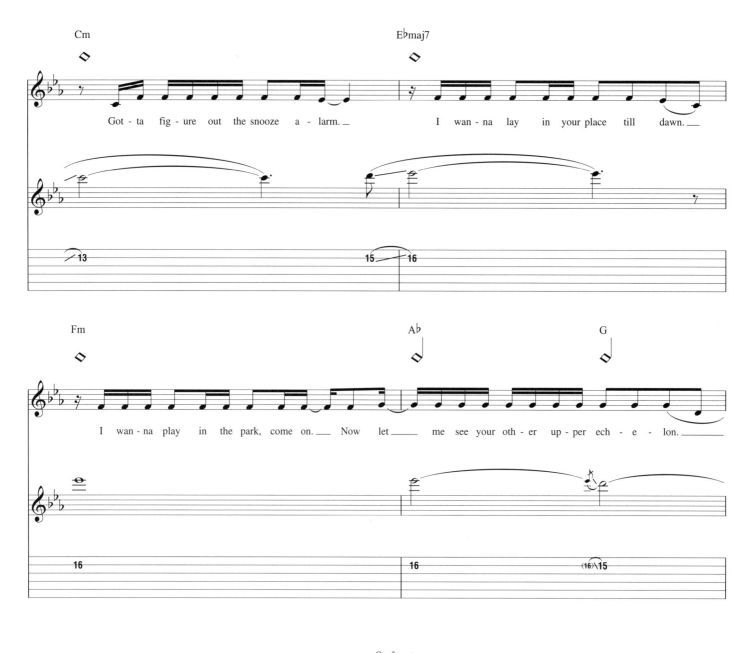

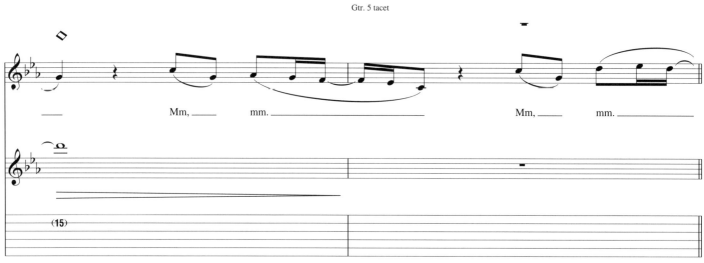

Pre-Chorus

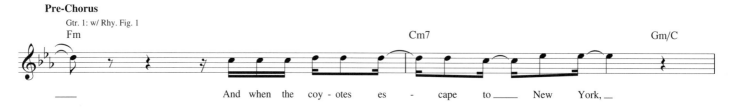

then the cit - y life _____ has crum - bled to the sea. _____

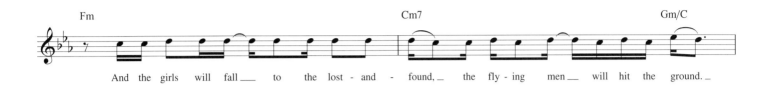

And the girls will fall _____ to the lost - and - found, _ the fly - ing men _____ will hit the ground. _

Ev - 'ry no - tion is clos - er to touch - ing. The coy - o - tes sing when they feast on your _ lov - ing. _

Gtr. 1: w/ Rhy. Fig. 2
Gtr. 3: w/ Riff A
Gtr. 4: w/ Riff B

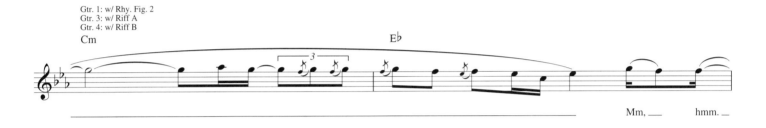

Mm, _____ hmm. _

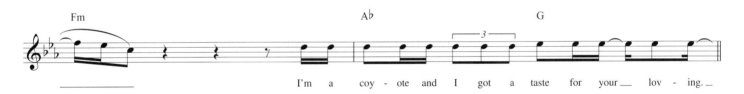

_____ I'm a coy - ote and I got a taste for your _ lov - ing. _

Outro-Chorus

Gtr. 1: w/ Rhy. Fig. 2 (5 times)
Gtr. 3: w/ Riff A (5 times)
Gtr. 4: w/ Riff B (5 times)

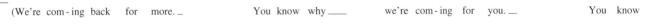

(We're com - ing back for more. _ You know why _____ we're com - ing for you. _ You know

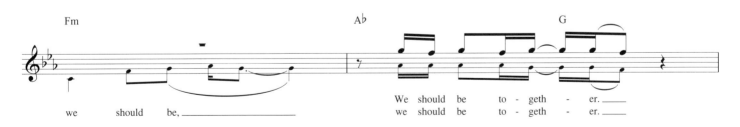

we should be, _____
We should be to - geth - er. _____
we should be to - geth - er. _____

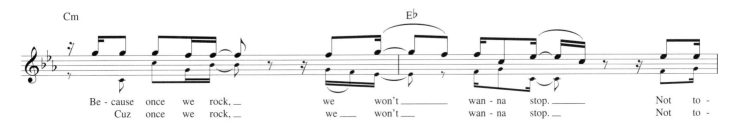

Be - cause once we rock, _ we won't _ wan - na stop. _ Not to -
Cuz once we rock, _ we won't _ wan - na stop. _ Not to -

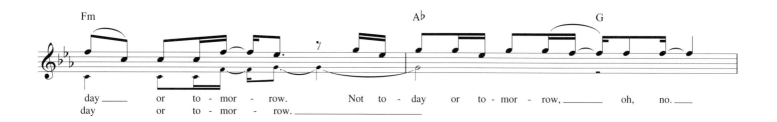

day _____ or to - mor - row.   Not to - day   or to - mor - row, _____ oh,   no. _____
day   or to - mor - row. _____

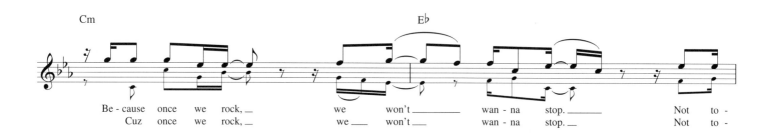

Be - cause once we rock, __   we   won't _____ wan - na stop. _____   Not   to -
Cuz once we rock, __   we __ won't _____ wan - na stop. __   Not   to -

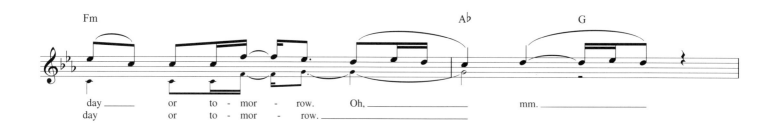

day _____ or to - mor - row.   Oh, _____   mm. _____
day   or to - mor - row. _____

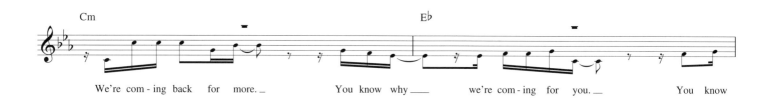

We're com - ing back   for more. __   You know why _____ we're com - ing for you. __   You know

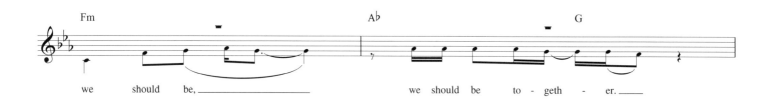

we   should be, _____   we should be to - geth - er. _____

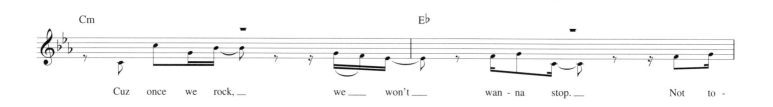

Cuz once we rock, __   we __ won't _____ wan - na stop. __   Not   to -

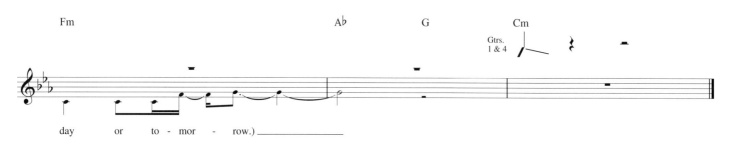

Gtrs.
1 & 4

day   or to - mor - row.) _____

ONLY HUMAN

Words and Music by
Jason Mraz and Sacha Skarbek

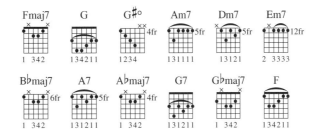

*Chord symbols reflect overall harmony.

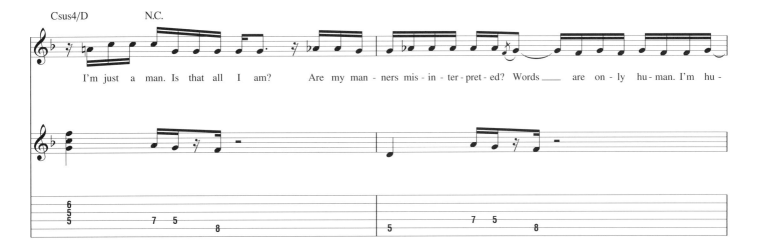

C/D   N.C.

-man. Made of flesh,__ made of sand,__ just like you,__ man.__

(cont. in slashes)

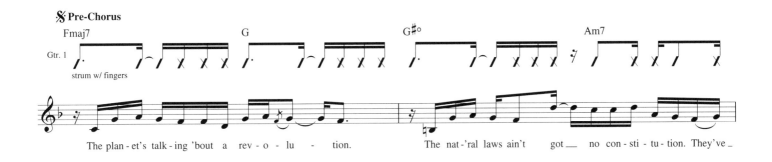

𝄋 Pre-Chorus

Fmaj7   G   G#°   Am7

Gtr. 1
strum w/ fingers

The plan-et's talk-ing 'bout a rev-o-lu - tion.   The nat-'ral laws ain't got__ no con-sti-tu-tion. They've__

Dm7   Em7

(cont. in notation)

got a right__ to live their own life.   But we keep pav-ing o-ver par-a-dise.__ 'Cause we're on - ly hu-

Chorus

N.C.   Dm7   N.C.   Fmaj7

-man.__   Oh yes, we are._____   On - ly hu-

Gtr. 1   **Rhy. Fig. 1**

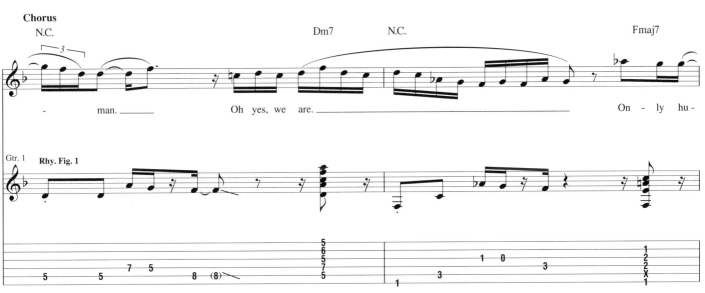

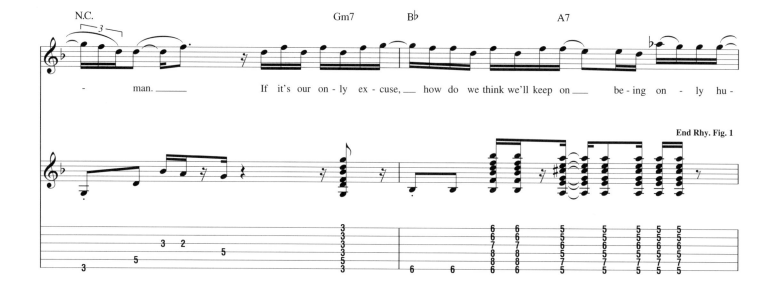

-man.   If it's our on - ly ex - cuse, ___ how do we think we'll keep on ___ be - ing on - ly hu-

Gtr. 1: w/ Rhy. Fig. 1

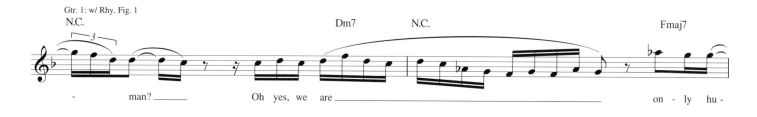

-man? ___   Oh yes, we are ___ on - ly hu-

To Coda

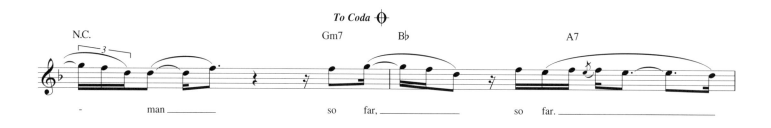

-man ___ so far, ___ so far. ___

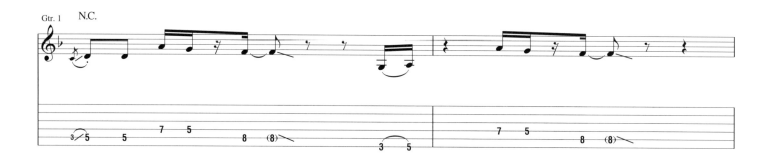

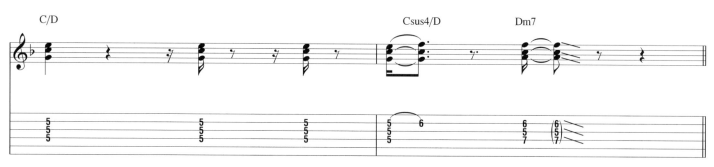

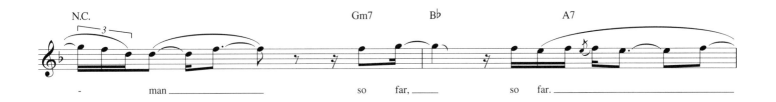

- man _____ so far, ___ so far. _____

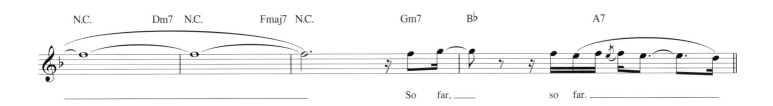

_____ So far, ___ so far. _____

Outro

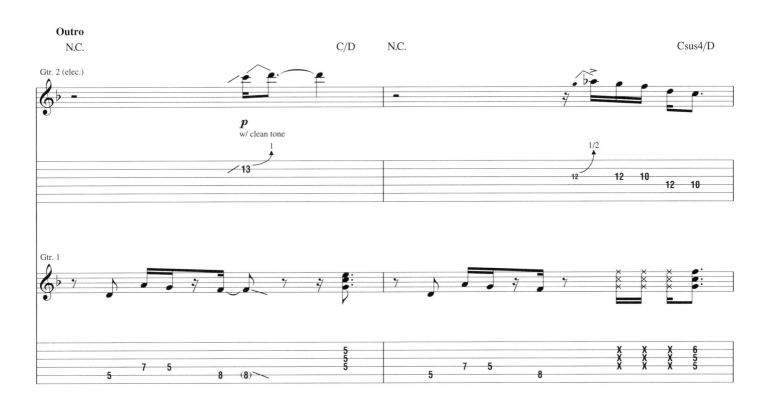

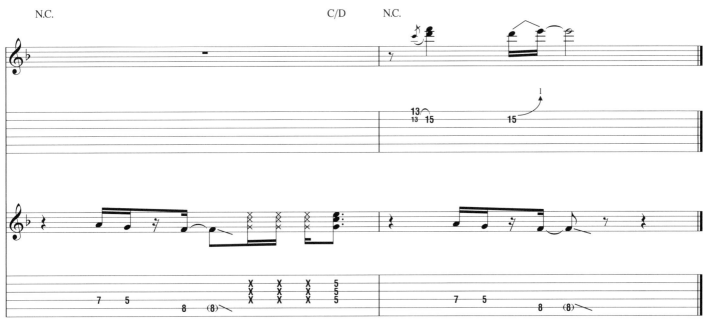

THE DYNAMO OF VOLITION

Words and Music by
Jason Mraz

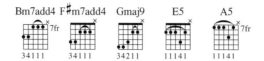

Gtr. 1 tuning:
(low to high) D-A-D-G-A-E

Verse
Moderate Funk ♩ = 118

1. I got the dy-na-mo of vo-li-tion, the p - pole po-si-tion, au-to-mat-ic trans-mis-sion with l - low e-mis-sions. I'm a

brand - new ad-di-tion to the old e-di-tion with a love un-con-di-tion-al. And I'm a

dra-ma ab-o-li-tion-ist, damn,_ no op-po-si-tion to my prop-o-si-tion. Half of a man,_ half ma-gi-cian. Half a

pol-i-ti-cian hold-ing the mic_ like am-mu-ni-tion, and my vi-sion is as sim-ple as light. Ain't no

rea-son we should be in a fight,_ no dem-o-li-tion. Get to vote, get to say what you like,_ pro - cre-a-tion. Com-po-

si-tions al-read-y writ-ten by them-selves. ___ Heck is for the peo-ple not be-liev-ing in gosh. ___ Good job. ___

Chorus

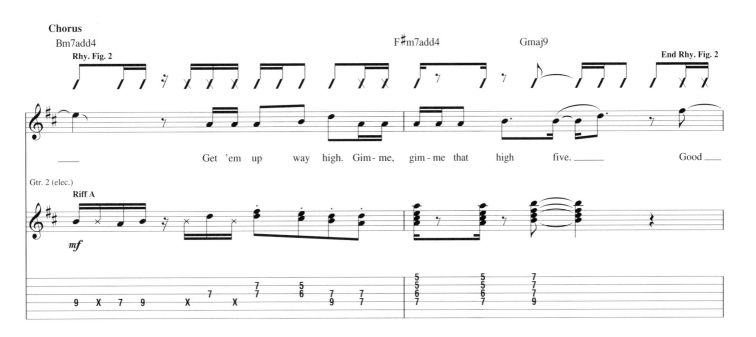

___ Get 'em up way high. Gim-me, gim-me that high five. ___ Good ___

___ times. ___ Get 'em way down low. ___ Gim-me, gim-me that low dough. ___ Good ___

___ God. ___ Bring 'em back a-gain. ___ Gim-me, gim-me that high ten. ___ You're the

83

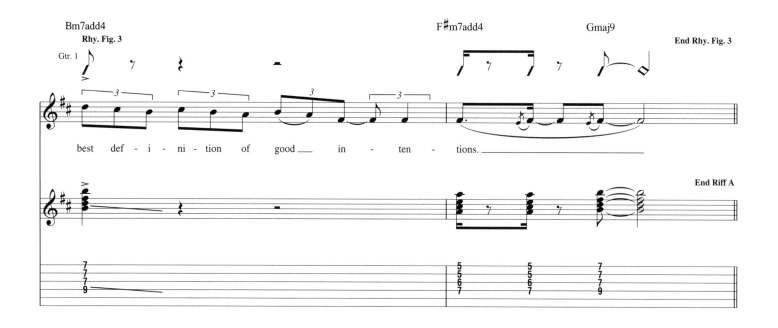

best def - i - ni - tion of good ___ in - ten - tions. ___

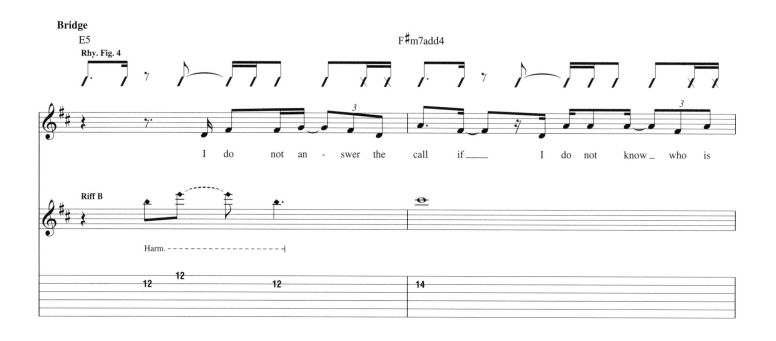

Bridge

I do not an - swer the call if ___ I do not know ___ who is

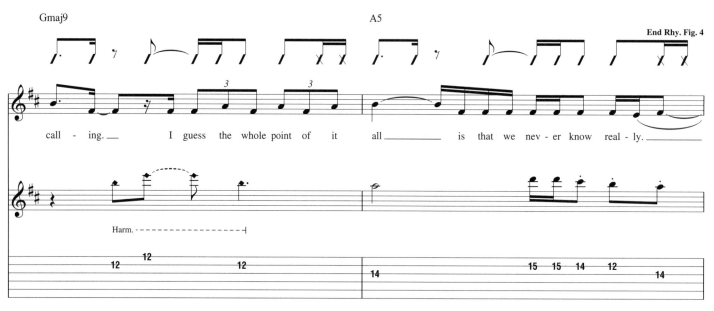

call - ing. ___ I guess the whole point of it all ___ is that we nev - er know real - ly. ___

Gtr. 1: w/ Rhy. Fig. 4

E5 · · · F#m7add4

I'm try'ng to keep ___ with the Jones - es ___ while wait - ing for guns and the

Harm. - - - - - - - - - - -

Gmaj9 · · · A5

ros - es ___ to fin - ish what we all sup - pose ___ is gon - na be the shit, as -

End Riff B

Harm. - - - - - - - - - - - - - -

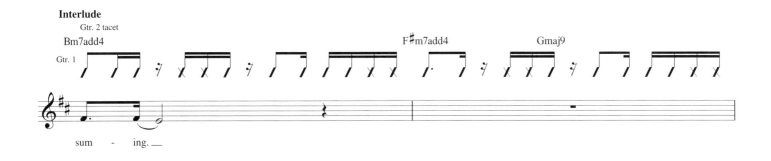

Interlude

Gtr. 2 tacet

Bm7add4 · · · F#m7add4 · · · Gmaj9

Gtr. 1

sum - ing. ___

Bm7add4 · · · F#m7add4 · · · Gmaj9

2. Oh,

Synth bass arr. for gtr.

mf

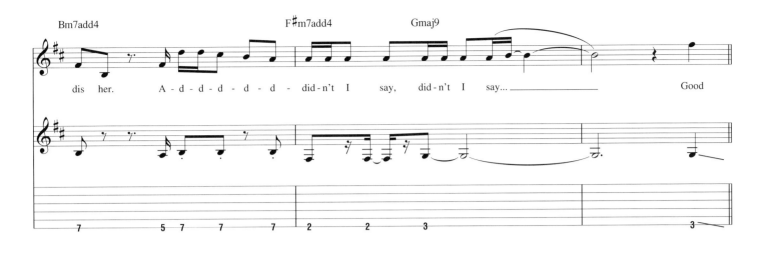

dis her. A - d - d - d - d - d - d - did-n't I say, did-n't I say... Good

Chorus

Gtr. 1: w/ Rhy. Fig. 2 (3 times)
Gtr. 2: w/ Riff A

job. Get 'em up way high. Gim - me, gim - me that high five. Good

times. Get 'em way down low. Gim - me, gim - me that low dough. Good

God. Bring 'em back a - gain. Gim - me, gim - me that high ten. You're the

Gtr. 1: w/ Rhy. Fig. 3

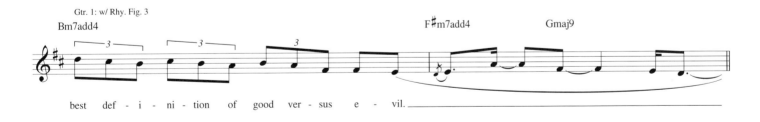

best def - i - ni - tion of good ver - sus e - vil.

Verse

Rhy. Fig. 5

End Rhy. Fig. 5

Gtr. 1

3. I do not keep up with sta - tis - tics. I do not sleep with - out a

Gtr. 1: w/ Rhy. Fig. 5 (3 times)

Bm7add4   F#m7add4   Gmaj9

mis - tress.   I   do   not   eat   un - less   it's fixed   with   some   kind   of   sweet   like   a

Bm7add4   F#m7add4   Gmaj9

lic - 'rice.   My   home   is   deep   in - side   the   mys - tics.   I'm   known   to   keep   dig - ging   on   ex -

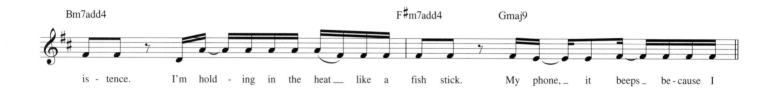

Bm7add4   F#m7add4   Gmaj9

is - tence.   I'm   hold - ing   in   the   heat   like   a   fish   stick.   My   phone,   it   beeps   be - cause   I

Bridge

Gtr. 1: w/ Rhy. Fig. 4 (3 1/2 times)
Gtr. 2: w/ Riff B (1st 4 meas., 2 times)

E5   F#m7add4

missed   it.   I   do   not   an - swer   the   call   if   I   do   not   know   who   is

Gmaj9   A5

call - ing.   I'm   mak - ing   no   sense   of   it   all.   Say,   can   I   get   a   wit - ness.

E5   F#m7add4

I'm   on - ly   a   boy   in   a   sto - ry,   just   a   ha - lu - cin - a -

Gmaj9   A5

to - ry   trip - ping   on   noth - ing   there   is,   liv - ing   in   the   wil - der - ness.

Gtr. 2: w/ Riff B

E5 — F#m7add4 — With a ti-ger spot on my __ back, liv-ing life __ of a __

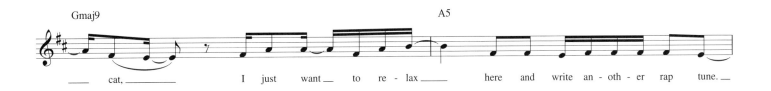

Gmaj9 — A5 — __ cat, __ I just want __ to re-lax __ here and write an-oth-er rap tune. __

E5 — F#m7add4 — __ Driv - ing off __ on your blind man's bike, you can

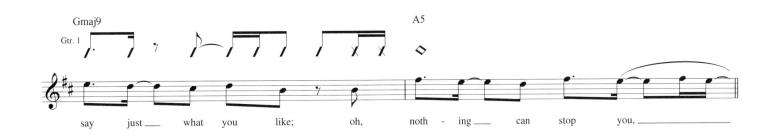

Gmaj9 — Gtr. 1 — A5 — say just __ what you like; oh, noth-ing __ can stop you, __

Interlude

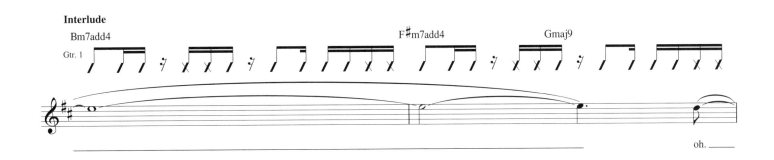

Bm7add4 — Gtr. 1 — F#m7add4 — Gmaj9 — oh. __

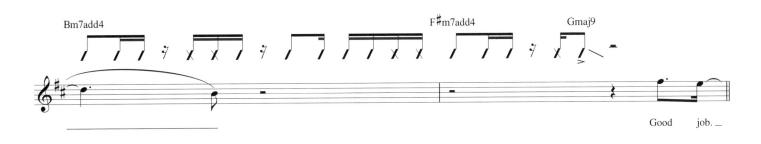

Bm7add4 — F#m7add4 — Gmaj9 — Good job. __

Chorus

Gtr. 1: w/ Rhy. Fig. 2 (3 times)
Gtr. 2: w/ Riff A (2 times)

_____ Get 'em up way high. Gim - me, gim - me that high five. _____ Good _

_____ times. _____ Get 'em way down low. __ Gim - me, gim - me that low __ dough. _____ Good _

_____ God. _____ Bring 'em back a - gain. __ Gim - me, gim - me that high ten. _____ You're the

Gtr. 1: w/ Rhy. Fig. 3

best, you're the best, you're the best, you're the best, you're the best, you're the best, you're the best. Good job. _

Gtr. 1: w/ Rhy. Fig. 2 (3 times)

_____ Get 'em up way high. Gim - me, gim - me that high five. _____ Good _

_____ times. _____ Get 'em way down low. __ Gim - me, gim - me that low dough. _ Good _

Bm7add4   F#m7add4   Gmaj9

____ God. ____ Bring 'em back a - gain. ____ Gim - me, gim - me that high ten. ____ You're the

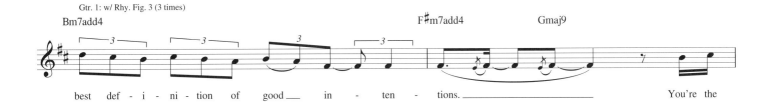

Gtr. 1: w/ Rhy. Fig. 3 (3 times)

Bm7add4   F#m7add4   Gmaj9

best def - i - ni - tion of good ___ in - ten - tions. ____ You're the

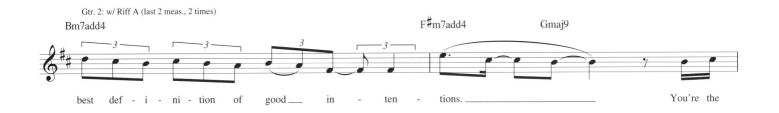

Gtr. 2: w/ Riff A (last 2 meas., 2 times)

Bm7add4   F#m7add4   Gmaj9

best def - i - ni - tion of good ___ in - ten - tions. ____ You're the

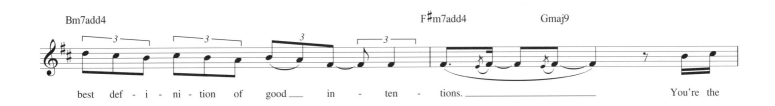

Bm7add4   F#m7add4   Gmaj9

best def - i - ni - tion of good ___ in - ten - tions. ____ You're the

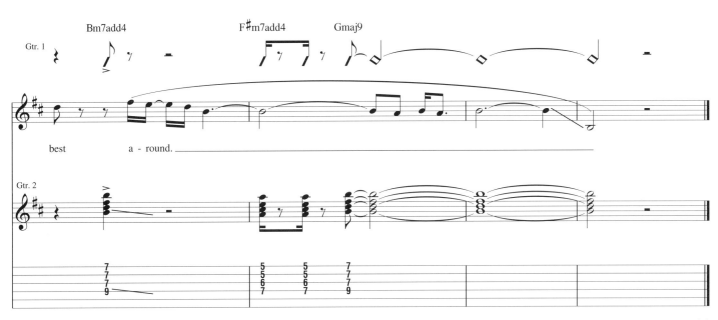

best a - round. ____

IF IT KILLS ME

Words and Music by
Jason Mraz, Martin Terefe and
Sacha Skarbek

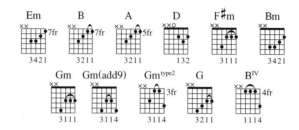

Intro
Moderately ♩ = 72

Verse

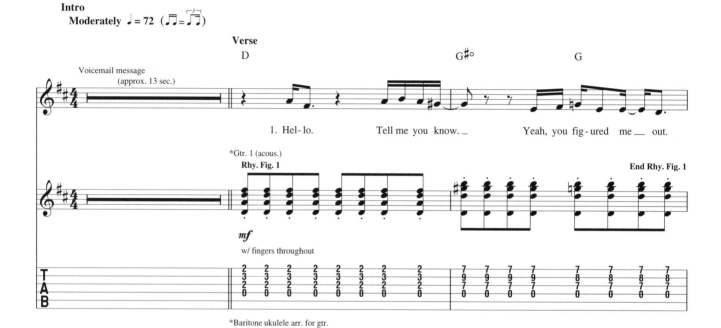

1. Hel- lo. Tell me you know. _ Yeah, you fig- ured me _ out.

*Gtr. 1 (acous.)
Rhy. Fig. 1
End Rhy. Fig. 1
mf
w/ fingers throughout

*Baritone ukulele arr. for gtr.

Gtr. 1: w/ Rhy. Fig. 1 (3 times)

Some - thing gave it a - way. _

It would be _ such a beau-ti-ful mo - ment to see the look on your _ face.

To know that I know that you know _ now. _

Gtr. 1: w/ Rhy. Fig. 3

D   F#m

And all I real - ly want from you is to feel ___ me   as the feel - ing in - side ___ keeps build -

Bm   Gm Gm(add9) Gm^{type2} Gm

- ing. ___ And I will find a way to you if it kills ___ me,   if it kills ___ me.

D   Gm Gm(add9) Gm   End Rhy. Fig. 4

Rhy. Fig. 4

Gtr. 1

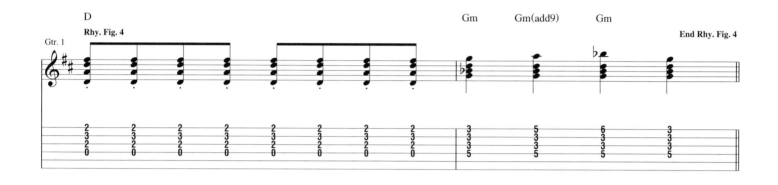

Verse

Gtr. 1: w/ Rhy. Fig. 1 (4 times)

D   G#°   G

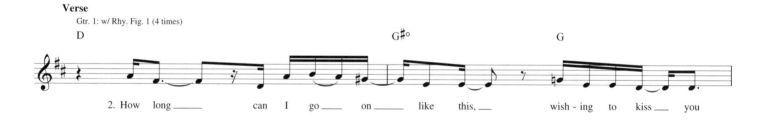

2. How long ___ can I go ___ on ___ like this, ___ wish - ing to kiss ___ you

D   G#° G   D

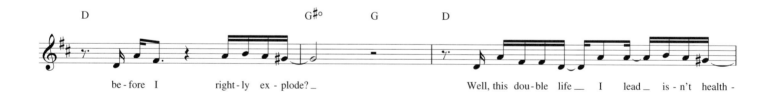

be - fore I right - ly ex - plode? ___   Well, this dou - ble life ___ I lead ___ is - n't health -

G#°   G   D   G#° G

- y for me; in fact, it makes me nerv - ous.   If I get ___ caught I could be risk - ing it all. ___

Gtr. 1: w/ Rhy. Fig. 2

Em   B   Em B A

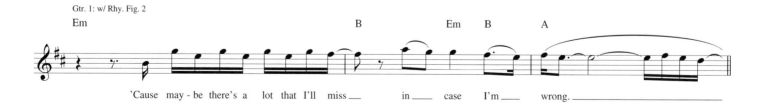

'Cause may - be there's a lot that I'll miss ___ in ___ case I'm ___ wrong. ___

Chorus

Gtr. 1: w/ Rhy. Fig. 3 (2 times)

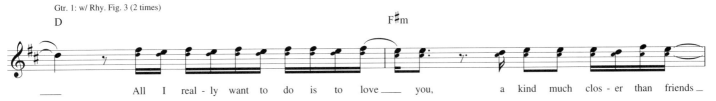

All I real-ly want to do is to love ___ you, a kind much clos-er than friends ___

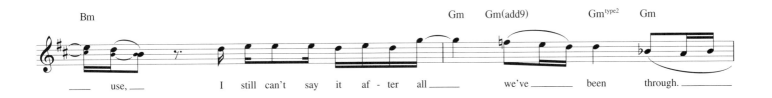

___ use, ___ I still can't say it af-ter all ___ we've ___ been through. ___

___ And all I real-ly want from you is to feel ___ me as the feel-ing in-side ___ keeps build-

-ing. ___ And I will find a way to you if it kills ___ me, if it kills ___ me, if it kills ___

Bridge

Gtr. 1: w/ Rhy. Fig. 4

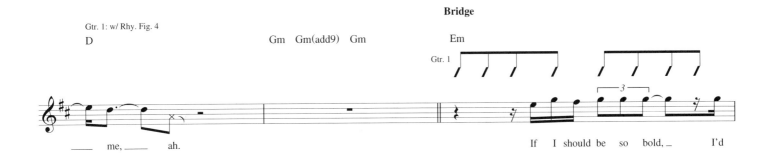

___ me, ___ ah. If I should be so bold, ___ I'd

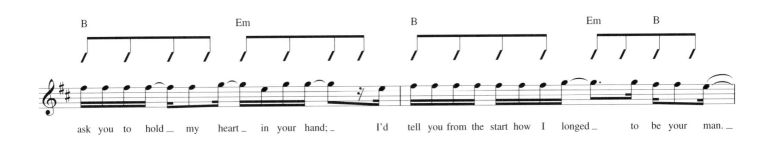

ask you to hold ___ my heart ___ in your hand; ___ I'd tell you from the start how I longed ___ to be your man. ___

But I nev-er said a word. I guess I've gone and missed my chance a-gain. _

D   F#m   G   Gm   Gm(add9) Gm^type2 Gm

Chorus
Gtr. 1: w/ Rhy. Fig. 3 (2 times)

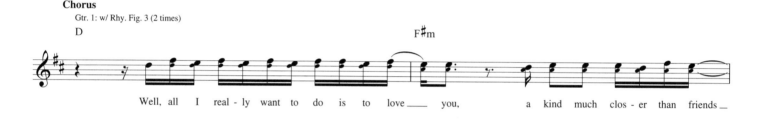

D   F#m

Well, all I real-ly want to do is to love ___ you, a kind much clos-er than friends ___

Bm   Gm   Gm(add9)   Gm^type2   Gm

___ use, ___ I still can't say it af-ter all _____ we've _____ been through. _____

D   F#m

___ And all I real-ly want from you is to feel ___ me as the feel-ing in-side ___ keeps build-

Bm   Gm   Gm(add9)   Gm^type2   Gm

-ing. ___ And I will find a way to you if it kills ___ me, if it kills ___ me, if it kills ___

Outro

Gtr. 1: w/ Rhy. Fig. 3 (1 1/2 times)

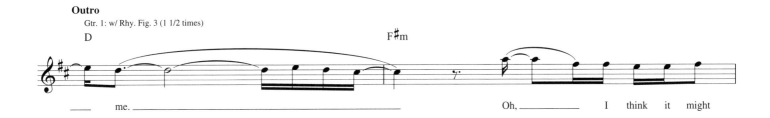

____ me. _____ Oh, _____ I think it might

kill ____ me.

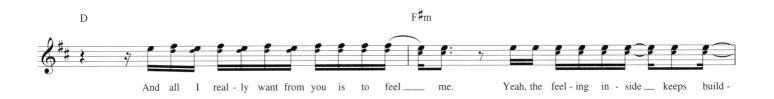

And all I real-ly want from you is to feel ____ me. Yeah, the feel-ing in-side ____ keeps build-

- ing. I'll find a way to you if it kills ____ me, if it kills ____ me. It might kill ____

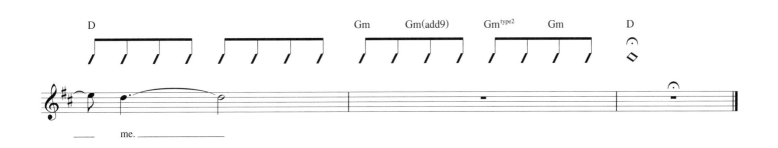

____ me. _____

A BEAUTIFUL MESS

Words and Music by
Jason Mraz, Mona Tavakoli, Chaska Potter,
Mai Bloomfield and Becky Gebhard

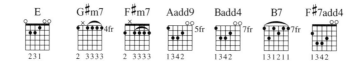

Intro
Slowly, in 2 ♩ = 40

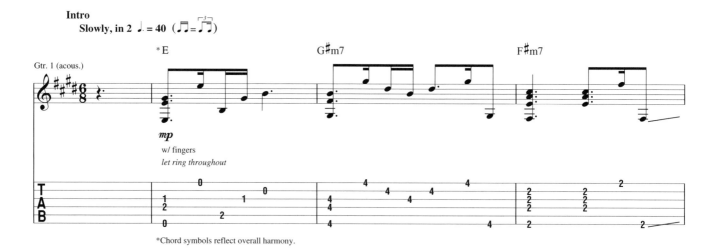

*Chord symbols reflect overall harmony.

Verse

1. You got the best of both worlds; ___

Rhy. Fig. 1

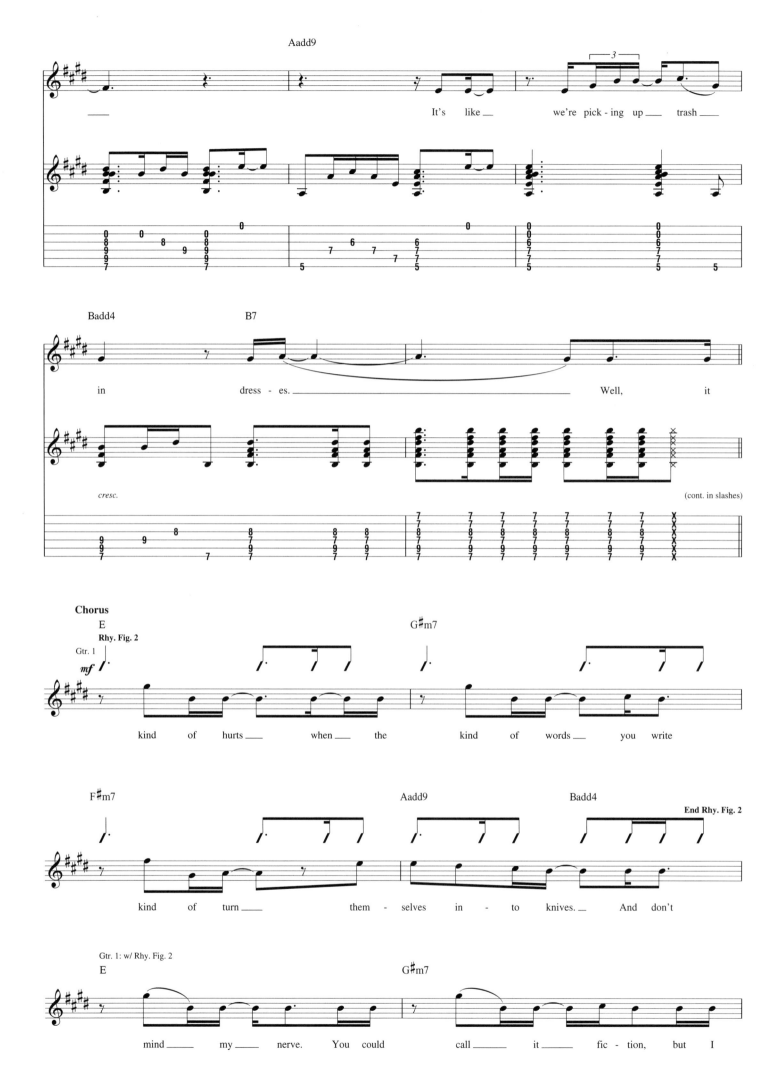

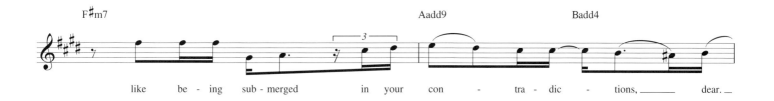

like be - ing sub - merged in your con - tra - dic - tions, _____ dear. _____

'Cause here _____ we are, _____

here we

are.

*Fret 6th-string notes w/ thumb (next 3 meas.).

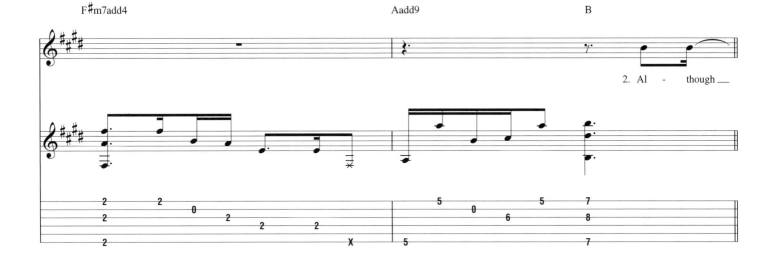

Verse

Gtr. 1: w/ Rhy. Fig. 1 (2 times)

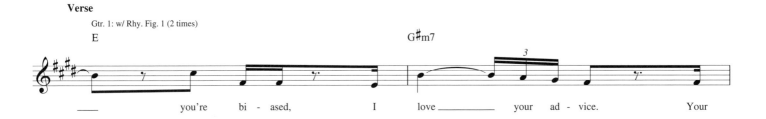

_____ you're bi - ased, I love _____ your ad - vice. Your

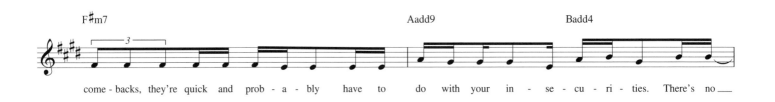

come - backs, they're quick and prob - a - bly have to do with your in - se - cu - ri - ties. There's no ___

___ shame in be - ing cra - zy, de - pend - ing on how you take these

words I'm par - a - phras - ing, this re - la - tion - ship we're ___ stag - ing. ___

Pre-Chorus

Gtr. 1

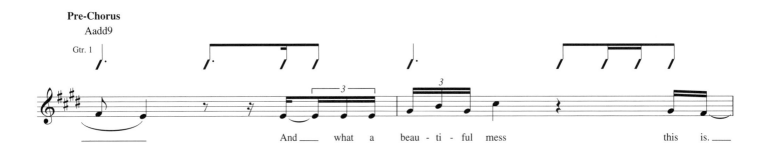

_____ And ___ what a beau - ti - ful mess this is. ___

Badd4   Aadd9

It's like ___

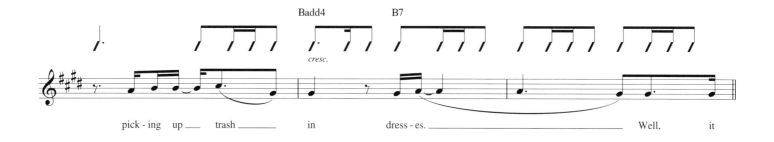

                                    Badd4   B7

pick - ing up ___ trash ___ in dress - es. ___ Well, it

Chorus
Gtr. 1: w/ Rhy. Fig. 2 (2 times)

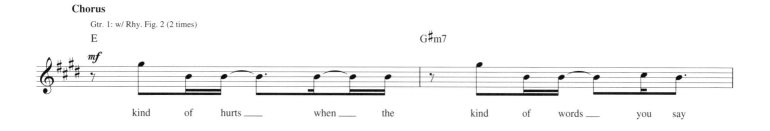

E   G#m7

kind of hurts ___ when ___ the kind of words ___ you say

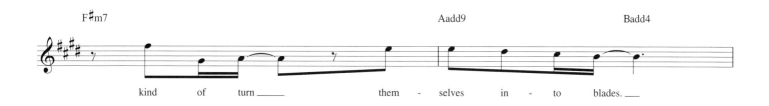

F#m7   Aadd9   Badd4

kind of turn ___ them - selves in - to blades. ___

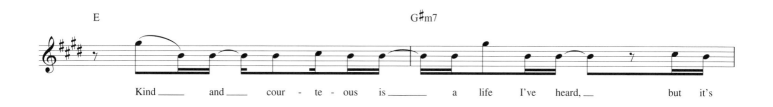

E   G#m7

Kind ___ and ___ cour - te - ous is ___ a life I've heard, ___ but it's

F#m7   Aadd9   Badd4

nice to say ___ that we played in the dirt, ___ oh, ___ dear. ___

'Cause here _____ we are, _____ here we are. _____

Bridge

Here we are. __ Here we are. __ Here we are. _____

(Here we are. __ Here we are. __ Here we are. __ Here we are. _____

Here we are. __ We're still here. _____

Here we are. __ Here we are. __ Here we are. __ We're still here.) _____

Pre-Chorus

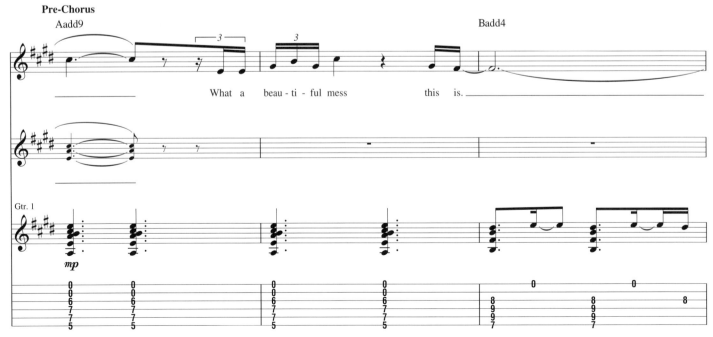

What a beau-ti-ful mess this is. _____

Aadd9

It's like ___ tak - ing a guess ___ when the

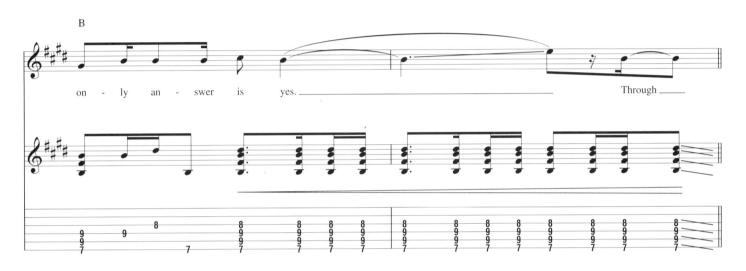

B

on - ly an - swer is yes. _____ Through ___

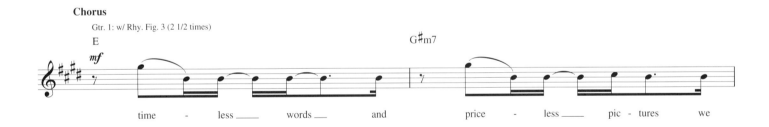

Chorus

Gtr. 1: w/ Rhy. Fig. 3 (2 1/2 times)

E   G#m7

time - less ___ words ___ and   price - less ___ pic - tures we

F#m7   Aadd9   Badd4

fly   like ___ birds ___   not   of   this   earth. ___   And

E   G#m7

tides ___ they ___ turn ___   and   hearts ___ dis - fig - ure,   but   that's

no con - cern _____ when we're wound - ed to - geth - er. And we

tore our dress - es and stained our shirts, _____ but it's

Freely

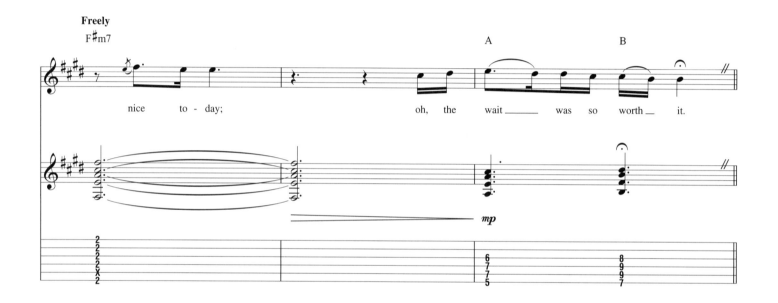

nice to - day; oh, the wait _____ was so worth _____ it.

Outro
Tempo I

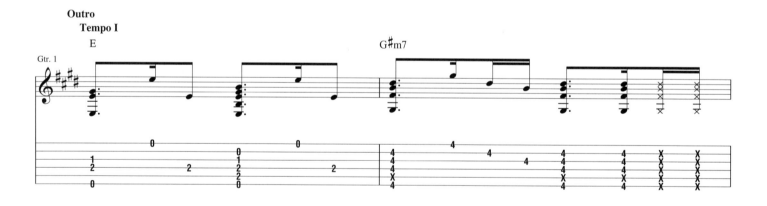

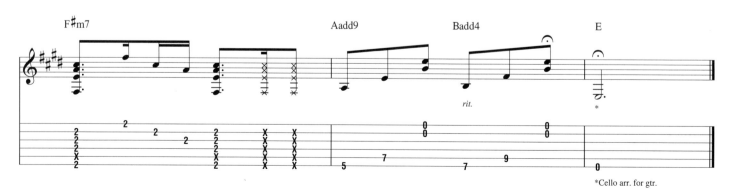

*Cello arr. for gtr.

Guitar Notation Legend

Guitar music can be notated three different ways: on a *musical staff*, in *tablature*, and in *rhythm slashes*.

RHYTHM SLASHES are written above the staff. Strum chords in the rhythm indicated. Use the chord diagrams found at the top of the first page of the transcription for the appropriate chord voicings. Round noteheads indicate single notes.

THE MUSICAL STAFF shows pitches and rhythms and is divided by bar lines into measures. Pitches are named after the first seven letters of the alphabet.

TABLATURE graphically represents the guitar fingerboard. Each horizontal line represents a string, and each number represents a fret.

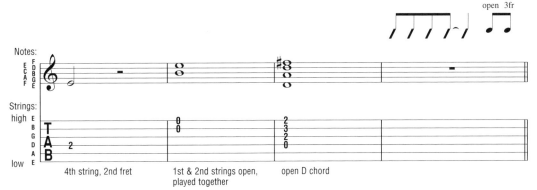

4th string, 2nd fret

1st & 2nd strings open, played together

open D chord

HALF-STEP BEND: Strike the note and bend up 1/2 step.

WHOLE-STEP BEND: Strike the note and bend up one step.

GRACE NOTE BEND: Strike the note and immediately bend up as indicated.

SLIGHT (MICROTONE) BEND: Strike the note and bend up 1/4 step.

BEND AND RELEASE: Strike the note and bend up as indicated, then release back to the original note. Only the first note is struck.

PRE-BEND: Bend the note as indicated, then strike it.

VIBRATO: The string is vibrated by rapidly bending and releasing the note with the fretting hand.

WIDE VIBRATO: The pitch is varied to a greater degree by vibrating with the fretting hand.

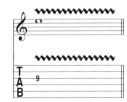

HAMMER-ON: Strike the first (lower) note with one finger, then sound the higher note (on the same string) with another finger by fretting it without picking.

PULL-OFF: Place both fingers on the notes to be sounded. Strike the first note and without picking, pull the finger off to sound the second (lower) note.

LEGATO SLIDE: Strike the first note and then slide the same fret-hand finger up or down to the second note. The second note is not struck.

SHIFT SLIDE: Same as legato slide, except the second note is struck.

TRILL: Very rapidly alternate between the notes indicated by continuously hammering on and pulling off.

TAPPING: Hammer ("tap") the fret indicated with the pick-hand index or middle finger and pull off to the note fretted by the fret hand.

NATURAL HARMONIC: Strike the note while the fret-hand lightly touches the string directly over the fret indicated.

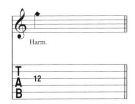

PINCH HARMONIC: The note is fretted normally and a harmonic is produced by adding the edge of the thumb or the tip of the index finger of the pick hand to the normal pick attack.

PICK SCRAPE: The edge of the pick is rubbed down (or up) the string, producing a scratchy sound.

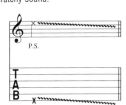

MUFFLED STRINGS: A percussive sound is produced by laying the fret hand across the string(s) without depressing, and striking them with the pick hand.

PALM MUTING: The note is partially muted by the pick hand lightly touching the string(s) just before the bridge.

RAKE: Drag the pick across the strings indicated with a single motion.

TREMOLO PICKING: The note is picked as rapidly and continuously as possible.

VIBRATO BAR DIVE AND RETURN: The pitch of the note or chord is dropped a specified number of steps (in rhythm), then returned to the original pitch.

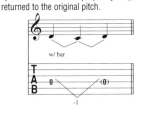

VIBRATO BAR SCOOP: Depress the bar just before striking the note, then quickly release the bar.

VIBRATO BAR DIP: Strike the note and then immediately drop a specified number of steps, then release back to the original pitch.

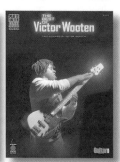